The Dudwell School
Cookbook

Caroline Waldegrave

First published in Great Britain in 2020 by Dudwell School Ltd

DISCLAIMER: Cooking and eating involve inherent dangers. Please only undertake activities that you believe to be safe and comfortable. Dudwell School Ltd and Caroline Waldegrave assume no responsibility or liability for any damages you may experience as a result of following these recipes. All dietary indications in the recipes are a starting point for your own review, not an absolute statement of vegetarian, wheat-free, gluten-free, dairy-free or sugar-free status.

Please pay particular attention to the safety notes found on pages 168–175 and within the individual recipes.

Produced by Tandem Publishing http://tandempublishing.yolasite.com/

ISBN 978 1 5272 5643 9

10 9 8 7 6 5 4 3 2 1

A CIP catalogue record for this book is available from the British Library.

Printed and bound in Great Britain by CPI Group (UK) Ltd, Croydon CR0 4YY

Introduction

If you understand the basics of cooking and the reason why you cook ingredients in different ways it will give you the confidence to tackle any recipe in any cookbook.

This collection of recipes includes enough skills and ideas for you to cook something for any occasion, from a student chilli supper to a grand dinner party. You will learn how to make pastry, bread and many sauces. You will be able to joint a chicken, fillet a fish and ice a cake. You will cook with spices and unusual ingredients and be able to make soufflés and macaroons. You will be able to make slow-cooked dishes and perfect hamburgers. But most importantly I hope you will learn to really enjoy cooking.

Before you start to cook, read the recipe so that you know what pieces of equipment you will need to have to hand.

Then look at the list of ingredients, and all the advance preparation required is in the ingredient list e.g. onion, finely chopped.

At the end of this booklet there are various general tips that you may find useful.

Several of the recipes here are adaptations of those found in *Leiths Cookery Bible* and *The Eton Cookbook*. A few have been adapted from other people's recipes; those chefs have been credited when I've remembered the source. Many apologies for any inadvertent omissions.

Have fun.

Photographs by
Toby Mather
Charlie Broad
Thomas Ward

Conversion Tables

All the recipes are in metric quantities. Many of the measurements are in spoon quantities and I would recommend owning a set of measuring spoons as they are absolutely accurate – spoons at home vary in size considerably. All spoon quantities are for a level spoon unless otherwise stated.

Dry Ingredients

I would recommend following the recipes in their metric quantities rather than converting them to pounds and ounces as it is reasonably difficult to do so. 1oz = 28.3g and it is all too easy to inadvertently alter the proportions of the ingredients. With most recipes it doesn't matter too much if you use too few or too many grams here and there, but when baking accuracy is key.

If you would like to convert your recipe the following table can be used as a guide.

METRIC	IMPERIAL		METRIC	IMPERIAL
15g	½oz		250–255g	9oz
25–30g	1oz		280–285g	10oz
55–60g	2oz		310–315g	11oz
80–85g	3oz		335–340g	12oz
110–115g	4oz		365–370g	13oz
140–145g	5oz		395–400g	14oz
165–170g	6oz		420–425g	15oz
195–200g	7oz		450–455g	16oz/1lb
225–230g	8oz			

Cup Quantities

Most American and Australian recipes give quantities in cups, which is a volume method of measurement. It is difficult to give an accurate conversion table for this, simply because it, in itself, is a slightly rough guide. For true accuracy, I would recommend weighing and measuring ingredients.

INGREDIENT	USA	METRIC
Flour	1 Cup	125g
Sugar and uncooked rice	1 Cup	170g
Butter	2 Sticks/1 Cup	225g
Dried fruit	1 Cup	140g
Ground almonds and chopped nuts	1 Cup	100g
Grated cheese	1 Cup	110g

INGREDIENT	AUSTRALIA	METRIC
Flour	1 Cup	140g
Sugar	1 Cup	170g
Uncooked rice	1 Cup	200g
Butter	1 Cup	225g
Dried Fruit	1 Cup	170g
Ground almonds and chopped nuts	1 Cup	110g
Grated Cheese	1 Cup	110g

Measurements

Most of the measurements are given in centimetres – should you wish to convert to inches divide by 2.5 and to convert from inches into centimetres multiply by 2.5, thus for example:

15cm = 6"

20cm = 8"

25cm = 10"

30cm = 12"

Liquid Conversions

The conversion from metric to imperial is difficult as 1 pint (20 fl oz) is 570ml (and note: an American pint is 16 fl oz and 473ml).

IMPERIAL	ML	AMERICAN CUPS
½ fl oz/1 tablespoon	15ml	
1 fl oz/2 tablespoons	30ml	1/8 cup
4 fl oz	120ml	½ cup (USA ¼ pint)
5 fl oz (¼ pint)	150ml	
8 fl oz	240ml	1 cup (USA ½ pint)
10 fl oz (½ pint)	290ml	
15 fl oz (¾ pint)	425ml	
20 fl oz (1 pint)	570ml	

WINE QUANTITIES	ML
1 wine glass	100ml

Oven Temperatures

All the recipes are given in degrees Celsius and Fahrenheit and gas temperature required. If using an Aga, owners tend to know 'their Aga'. The ovens and hotplates are maintained at different, but constant, temperatures so the first step is to choose the right oven of the Aga to cook in. The temperature can be reduced by placing large pans of very cold water on the hot plates; this gradually brings down the temperature within the ovens.

Fan assisted ovens are usually set approximately 25 degrees Celsius (i.e. approximately 50 degrees Fahrenheit) lower than others and cooking time is reduced by 10 minutes for every hour of cooking time. When baking dense cakes such as fruit cakes, it may be necessary to cover the top of the cake half an hour or so before the cake is due to come out of the oven. If there is a single item in the oven the heat is all directed to that one item and the heat can become a little intense. When baking buns and scones the heat is evenly dispersed and they cook well.

Different manufacturers and oven types do vary, so always refer to your cooker instruction book.

All recipes serve 4 people unless otherwise stated.

Butter is salted unless otherwise stated.

Degrees Fahrenheit	Degrees Celsius	Gas Mark	Description
225	110	¼	Very Slow
250	120/130	½	Very Slow
275	140	1	Slow
300	150	2	Slow
325	160/170	3	Moderate
350	180	4	Moderate
375	190	5	Moderately Hot
400	200	6	Moderately Hot
425	220	7	Hot
450	230	8	Hot
475	240	9	Very Hot

First Courses and Snacks

Cheese Soufflé

Serves 2–3 as a main course or 4–6 as a first course. This recipe can be made using 4 largeish or 6 smaller ramekins or 1 x 15cm soufflé dish.

melted butter for greasing

dried white breadcrumbs

35g butter, salted

30g flour, plain

½ teaspoon dry English mustard

pinch of cayenne pepper

280ml milk

100g strong Cheddar, finely grated

4 medium eggs, separated

salt and freshly ground black pepper

1. Preheat the oven to 200C/400F, gas mark 6. Place a baking sheet on the top shelf of the oven (note: make sure there is enough space for the soufflé to rise).

2. Brush the soufflé dish or ramekins with melted butter and dust with the breadcrumbs.

3. Melt the 35g butter in a saucepan, add the flour, cayenne pepper and mustard, mix well and cook over a gentle heat for 45 seconds.

4. Remove from the heat and gradually add about half of the milk, stirring continually. When the mixture is smooth return to the heat and bring slowly up to the boil, stirring all the time and adding the remaining milk. Boil for one minute. The mixture will get thick and leave the sides of the pan.

5. Remove from the heat and add the grated cheese. Pile into a mixing bowl and when slightly cooled add the egg yolks and season with salt and pepper. It should be very well seasoned – the flavour will be diluted by the addition of the egg whites.

6. Whisk the egg whites until stiff but not dry. Beat a spoonful of the egg whites into the soufflé base. This is to 'loosen' the mixture and makes the folding in of the whites simpler than it otherwise would be. Fold in the remaining whites and pile into the soufflé dish or ramekins. If using a soufflé dish it should be just over three-quarters full – if using ramekins they should be full. Run your finger around the top of the mixture. This will give a 'top hat' appearance to the cooked soufflé. Tap the dish lightly on the work surface to remove any pockets of air.

7. Bake in the oven on the preheated baking sheet for 25–30 minutes for a

large soufflé or 8–10 minutes for individual soufflés. Serve immediately. (Do not test to see if the soufflé is cooked until two-thirds of the way through the cooking time. Then give the dish a slight shove – if it wobbles alarmingly cook for a further 5 minutes.)

Note: Individual soufflés can be made in advance and then frozen. Cook from frozen for one and a half times the normal recipe. I suggest testing this in your own oven before doing it for a dinner party.

Rocket Salsa Bruschetta

60g rocket, washed and coarsely chopped

2 tablespoons extra-virgin olive oil

½ small red onion, very finely chopped

1 tablespoon balsamic vinegar

2 ripe plum tomatoes, seeded and very finely chopped

10 kalamata olives, pitted and chopped

salt and freshly ground black pepper

For the bruschetta

2 ciabatta rolls, split in half horizontally

2 tablespoons extra-virgin olive oil

50g Parmesan cheese, freshly grated

1.	Mix all the ingredients for the salsa together and season well with salt and freshly ground black pepper. Set aside.

2.	Drizzle the olive oil over the cut side of the ciabatta rolls and grill lightly until golden brown.

3.	Sprinkle over the Parmesan cheese and grill again until the cheese just begins to colour.

4.	Divide the rocket salsa between the rolls and serve immediately whilst hot.

Thai Mussels

This recipe is quite spicy so if you prefer a mild curry reduce the amount of curry paste.

Serves 6

2kgs mussels, very well scrubbed

2 tablespoons oil

2 medium onions, very finely chopped

1 clove of garlic, crushed

1½ tablespoon red Thai curry paste

1 tablespoon chopped fresh coriander

150ml water or fish stock

1 tablespoon fish sauce

150ml coconut milk

salt

1.   Clean the mussels by scrubbing them well under a running tap. Pull away the 'beards' (seaweed-like threads). Throw away any mussels that are cracked, that remain open when tapped or feel very heavy for their size.

2.   Heat the oil in a large deep pan, add the onion and sweat until soft but not coloured. Add the garlic and curry paste and continue to cook for 45 seconds then add the stock or water and fish sauce, coconut milk and coriander and bring up to simmering point.

3.   Add the mussels, put on the lid and leave to steam over a low heat until the shells are open, shaking the pan occasionally (about 5 minutes). Tip the mussels into a colander set over a bowl.

4.   Warm a soup tureen or wide bowl.

5.   Throw away any mussels that have not opened. Pour the mussel liquid from the bowl into a saucepan. Boil and reduce well, season to taste with salt, if the sauce is too spicy add a little more coconut milk.

6.   Transfer the mussels to the soup tureen or wide bowl, pour over the sauce and sprinkle with the fresh coriander.

Red Onion Tarte Tatin

You will need a 20cm flan dish or a 20cm-deep loose-bottomed non-stick flan ring.

4 large red onions, peeled

knob of butter

1 tablespoon sunflower oil

25g caster sugar

good balsamic vinegar

375g puff pastry

For the garnish

sprig of fresh basil

1. Pre-heat the oven to 220C/425F, gas mark 7. Line the flan dish with silicone paper or 'Bake-O-Glide' paper. If using the flan ring you will not need to line it with paper but do bake the tatin on a baking sheet just in case it leaks a little.

2. Slice the onions into very thin segments (from pole to pole rather than round the equator). Leaving a tiny bit of the root intact will prevent the segments from breaking up.

3. Fry the onions gently in the butter and oil until they are soft and just beginning to colour, taking care that they remain as much as possible in segments. This will take about 15 minutes.

4. Arrange the onion segments in a decorative pattern in the bottom of the flan dish. Any that have broken up should be on the top layer. Sprinkle over the sugar and a good few splashes of balsamic vinegar. Allow to cool thoroughly.

5. Roll out the pastry quite thickly and cut to a circle exactly the size of the tin so that the pastry will fit snugly over the top of the onions. Once in place, prick the pastry all over with a fork, then allow the dish to rest in the refrigerator for half an hour.

6. Bake in the hot oven for 15 minutes until the pastry is well risen and colouring, then reduce the heat to 180C/350F, gas mark 4 for a further 10 minutes.

7. Once cooked, turn out the flan: place the serving plate on top of the flan and invert both together. Give a sharp shake down and away from yourself and remove the flan dish or ring. Peel off the paper and garnish with a sprig of fresh basil. Delicious eaten slightly warm.

Butternut Squash and Roquefort Salad

1 butternut squash, peeled and cut into 2.5cm/1" cubes

extra-virgin olive oil

ground cumin

dried chilli flakes

55g pine nuts, roasted

1 bag rocket & mixed leaves salad

juice of half a lemon

100g Roquefort, cubed

3 tablespoons pesto (see page 91)

1. Preheat the oven to 180C/350F, gas mark 4.

2. Put the pieces of squash into an oven-proof tray in a single layer. Drizzle lightly with olive oil. Then turn the squash to coat. Sprinkle sparingly with cumin and dried chilli flakes.

3. Place in the oven, on the middle shelf for 40 minutes.

4. Tip the salad leaves into a large, flattish-bottomed serving bowl.

5. Dress the leaves with the lemon juice and olive oil and toss.

6. Remove the squash from the oven and add to the leaves.

7. Scatter on crumbly cubes of cheese and drizzle over the pesto. Scatter over the pine nuts.

Roasted Tomato and Red Pepper Soup

This soup is delicious served hot or cold.

1kg ripe tomatoes, cut into quarters and seeded

2 red onions, cut into chunks

3 red peppers, seeded and cut into chunks

6 whole cloves garlic

chilli oil

sea salt

freshly ground black pepper

To serve cold

soured cream

chives, snipped

1. Preheat the oven to 200C/400F, gas mark 6.

2. Put the tomatoes, onions and peppers onto a baking sheet. Drizzle with chilli oil and season with salt and pepper – make sure the vegetables are coated in the oil. Bake for 10 minutes and add the garlic to the vegetables and bake for a further 30–40 minutes or until the vegetables are really soft.

3. Allow the vegetables to cool for a few minutes and then carefully remove the garlic and peel. Discard the skins.

4. Process the vegetables together in a food processor – this will have to be done in batches. The soup may need to be thinned with a little water or vegetable stock.

5. If serving the soup hot: tip into a saucepan, adjust the seasoning according to taste and re-heat. If serving cold: chill in the refrigerator and serve in individual bowls with soured cream and chives.

Ceviche

400g monkfish or sea bass, filleted, pin boned, skinned and diced

finely grated zest and juice of 2 limes

3 medium tomatoes, skinned, seeded and diced

2 small red chillies

½ red onion, very finely chopped

sea salt

2 tablespoons freshly chopped coriander

1 avocado, cut in half and sliced lengthways

4 tortillas, fried until crisp

sprigs of coriander

1.   Mix the fish with lime juice and leave in the refrigerator for 30 minutes.

2.   Add the tomatoes, lime zest, chillies, salt, onion and coriander.

3.   Serve with slices of avocado, tortillas and a sprig of coriander.

This is adapted from a recipe by Tom Parker Bowles.

Prawn Tempura

Please see the notes about deep-fat frying (page 161) before following this recipe. I would always recommend using an electric fryer for safety reasons. This recipe calls for raw shell-on prawns but if they are not available don't worry, just buy large raw prawns instead.

16 large, uncooked, shell-on prawns

plain flour

tempura batter mix

ice cold water

oil for deep-fat frying

For the dipping sauce

2 tablespoons soy sauce

1 teaspoon freshly grated ginger

2 tablespoons mirrin (Japanese rice vinegar)

1 tablespoon fish sauce

1. Prepare the prawns – if they are shell-on prawns remove the heads and shells but leave the tails on.

2. Run a sharp knife down the back of the prawns to remove the dark vein. Turn the prawns over and make a few small cuts on the flesh towards the vein side and press them flat – this will help to keep them straight whilst they are fried.

3. Simmer the ingredients for the dipping sauce very gently for 2 to 3 minutes. Pour into a small bowl and set aside.

4. Heat the oil in the fryer to 180C.

5. Dip the prawns into the plain flour and shake off any excess.

6. When the oil is hot – drop a little batter into the fryer – it should drop to the bottom and then rise up to the surface within 30 seconds or so.

7. Prepare the batter using ice cold water and following the manufacturer's instructions. The batter should be a little lumpy.

8. Dip the prepared prawns one at a time into the batter and drop them carefully into the fryer (see note) – do not over-fill the fryer – it may be necessary to cook them in two batches. Do not be tempted to put the prawns into the basket and lower them into the oil – all the batter will just stick to the basket. Cook for 3 minutes and then drain well on crumpled kitchen paper. Sprinkle lightly with salt and serve with the dipping sauce.

Note: If the first prawn sticks to the basket when you add the next one the best thing is to allow the prawn to 'swim' – hold the prawn with chopsticks or tongs near the top of the fryer and then partially submerge it in the fat and move it back and forth for 10 seconds or so. This will mean that the batter is set and thus it won't stick to the basket. Let go of the prawn and allow it to cook for 3 minutes.

Guacamole

Serves 4

1–3 fresh green chillies, seeded and chopped (according to how spicy you like your guacamole)

1 large clove of garlic, crushed

3 tablespoons fresh coriander leaves, roughly chopped

juice of 1 lime

2 ripe avocados, peeled, stoned and roughly chopped

1–2 spring onions, thinly sliced on the diagonal (optional)

salt and freshly ground black pepper

1. Mash the avocado pears with a fork – when soft, but with a rough texture, add the chillies, garlic, coriander and lime. Season to taste.

2. Add the spring onions.

Spinach Soufflé

Serves 2–3 as a main course or 4–6 as a first course. This recipe can be made using 4 largish or 6 smaller ramekins or 1 x 15cm soufflé dish.

melted butter for greasing

dried white breadcrumbs

35g butter

30g plain flour

½ teaspoon dry English mustard

a pinch of cayenne pepper

280ml milk

30g strong Cheddar, finely grated

200g spinach, wilted, seasoned, squeezed dry and finely chopped

4 medium eggs, separated

freshly grated nutmeg

salt and freshly ground black pepper

1.   Preheat the oven to 200C/400F, gas mark 6. Place a baking sheet on the top shelf of the oven (note: make sure there is enough space for the soufflé to rise).

2.   Brush the soufflé dish or ramekins with melted butter and dust with the breadcrumbs.

3.   Melt the 35g butter in a saucepan, add the flour, cayenne pepper and mustard, mix well and cook over a gentle heat for 45 seconds.

4.   Remove from the heat and gradually add the milk, stirring continually. Return to the heat and bring slowly up to the boil, stirring all the time. Boil for one minute. The mixture will get thick and leave the sides of the pan.

5.   Remove from the heat and add the grated cheese. When melted add the prepared spinach. Pile into a mixing bowl and when slightly cooled add the egg yolks and season with the nutmeg, salt and pepper. It should be very well seasoned – the flavour will be diluted by the addition of the egg whites.

6. Whisk the egg whites until stiff but not dry. Beat a spoonful of the egg whites into the soufflé base. This is to 'loosen' the mixture and makes the folding in of the whites simpler than it otherwise would be. Fold in the remaining whites and pile into the soufflé dish or ramekins. If using a soufflé dish it should be just over three-quarters full – if using ramekins they should be full. Run your finger around the top of the mixture. This will give a 'top hat' appearance to the cooked soufflé. Tap the dish lightly on the work surface to remove any pockets of air.

7. Bake in the oven on the preheated baking sheet for 25–30 minutes for a large soufflé or 8–10 minutes for individual soufflés. Serve immediately. (Do not test to see if the soufflé is cooked until two-thirds of the way through the cooking time. Then give the dish a slight shove – if it wobbles alarmingly cook for a further 5 minutes.)

Note: Individual soufflés can be made in advance and then frozen. Cook from frozen for one and a half times the normal recipe. I suggest testing this in your own oven before doing it for a dinner party.

Tomato, Avocado and Mozzarella Salad

If you can find burrata rather than mozzarella do use it as it is quite delicious – it is so soft that you can't slice it so simply place it in the middle of your serving dish and surround it with the slices of tomato and avocado pear.

2 tomatoes per person

½ avocado per person, sliced

55g mozzarella cheese per person, sliced

shredded fresh basil

French dressing (see page 90)

black olives

salt and freshly ground black pepper

1. Dip the tomatoes into boiling water for 10 seconds and then into cold water. Peel, and slice across the width into 1/8" thick slices, discarding both ends.

2. Arrange the tomato, avocado and cheese in overlapping slices on a serving dish.

3. Add the basil to the dressing. Pour over the salad and sprinkle with a few olives. Season well with salt and plenty of pepper.

Sushi

250g sushi rice

75ml mirrin (Japanese rice vinegar)

1 tablespoon caster sugar

1 teaspoon salt

2 eggs

1 tablespoon soy sauce

½ tablespoon oil

1 small cucumber

50g smoked salmon

1 avocado pear

vinegar

4 sheets of nori seaweed

wasabi (optional)

Small bunch of chives

For dipping

3 tablespoons soy sauce

1 red chilli seeded and finely chopped

To serve

wasabi

Japanese pickled ginger

1.   Cook the rice according to the manufacturer's instructions. Generally for 250g of rice you will need 350ml of water. Put the rice and water into a pan. Bring up to the boil – simmer for 10 minutes with the lid on. Remove from the heat and leave to stand, covered, for 15 minutes – do not uncover during the 15 minutes. All the water should have been absorbed – do not drain the rice.

2.   Meanwhile heat the mirrin with the sugar, add the salt and when dissolved remove from the heat and allow to cool.

3.   When the rice is cooked pile onto a flat plate, pour over the mirrin mixture and toss with a fork – take care as it is important that the rice grains remain separated. Allow to cool.

4.   Prepare the fillings. Beat the eggs and soy sauce together and season with pepper. Heat the oil in a non-stick frying pan and when hot add enough of the egg mixture to cover the base. When it is set carefully turn the omelette over and cook until just set. Repeat with the remaining egg mix. The omelettes should look more like crepes than omelettes. When cold cut into strips.

5.   Peel the cucumber. Cut in half lengthways and using a teaspoon remove all the seeds. Cut into fine lengths about the width of the nori seaweed.

6.   Cut the smoked salmon into strips.

7.   Peel and stone the avocado. Cut into strips as best you can.

8. Put some water into a mixing bowl and add a splash of vinegar.

9. Lay a sheet of nori seaweed on a sushi mat and press a layer of rice over the mat leaving a margin of about 1cm at each end. Your hands will get sticky so use the acidulated water to rinse them as required.

10. The sushi can now be filled as required. Arrange the fillings across the rice as tidily as you can. Do not over-fill – a couple of slices of smoked salmon, 1–2 pieces of cucumber, 2 strips of omelette and two pieces of avocado topped with 2 or 3 chives will be plenty for each roll.

11. Press the margin of sushi nearest to you over the rice and then using the sushi mat to help you roll up the sushi as tightly as you can. Dampen the end margin of nori as this will help to glue it in place. Once it looks neat wrap it in cling film and refrigerate for 15 minutes or so.

12. Mix the soy sauce with the chilli and put into a small bowl.

13. Place the wasabi in a second bowl.

14. Squeeze the ginger firmly and place in a third bowl.

15. Remove the sushi from the refrigerator and using a serrated-edge knife cut into 8 very even slices. The ends of the sushi will probably need to be discarded. Wipe the knife – if it gets sticky clean the knife with some very hot water – between cutting the slices.

16. Arrange on a large plate and hand the dipping sauce, wasabi and pickled ginger separately.

Quiche Lorraine

Serves 2–3. 170g rich shortcrust pastry (see page 148).

For the filling

15g butter

1 small onion, finely diced

100g streaky bacon, diced

170ml double cream

80ml milk

2 large eggs, beaten

salt and freshly ground black pepper

40g Cheddar cheese, finely grated

1.   Preheat the oven to 200C/400F, gas mark 6.

2.   Roll out the pastry and use it to line a 20cm flan ring, 4cm deep. Chill until firm and then bake blind. (See page 163.) There will be pastry leftover – save it in case you need to patch any cracks once the pastry has been baked. The pastry case must be cold before you add the filling.

3.   Preheat the oven to 150C/300F, gas mark 2.

4.   Make the filling: melt the butter in a small frying pan, add the onions and using a cartouche (a dampened piece of crumpled greaseproof paper) sweat until soft. This may take 30 minutes. Add the bacon, increase the heat and fry until the bacon is lightly browned. Remove from the pan with a slotted spoon and allow to cool.

5.   Mix together the cream, milk and eggs and pass through a sieve to remove any egg threads.

6.   Add half of the grated cheese. Season lightly – remember that both cheese and bacon are salty.

7.   Place the onion and bacon in the baked pastry case.

8.   Pour over the filling mixture until the flan is almost full, scatter the remaining

cheese over the filling and then very carefully place in the oven for 40–50 minutes. The quiche should feel just set and be a pale yellow colour.

9.   Serve warm or cold.

Note: A classic Quiche Lorraine does not have the addition of grated cheese but I think it makes it more delicious than one without any cheese.

Cheese Omelette

2 large eggs

salt and freshly ground black pepper

1 tablespoon cold water

20g freshly grated Cheddar cheese

10g unsalted butter

1. Break the eggs into a bowl and whisk with a fork until foamy and no longer streaky. Add the salt and pepper and water.

2. Melt the butter in a heavy 15cm non-stick frying pan and swirl it around so that the bottom and sides are coated. When foaming, add the egg mixture.

3. Hold the pan in your left hand and move it gently back and forth over the heat. At the same time, using a spatula (made for non-stick pans) and tilting the pan slowly, scrape up creamy flakes of egg mixture. As you do this, some of the liquid egg from the middle of the omelette will run to the sides of the pan. When the bottom has set and the top is creamy, scatter the cheese down the centre of the mixture and, just as it begins to melt, remove the pan from the heat.

4. Fold the nearside edge of the omelette over to the centre and do the same with the far side edge. Flick the omelette over onto a plate and serve immediately.

Leek and Potato Soup

This soup is delicious served hot or cold.

The recipe calls for 500g leeks, white part only – to achieve this you will need to buy about 750g leeks.

70g butter

500g leeks, white part only, washed and chopped

1 large onion, finely chopped

300g floury potatoes, washed

750ml chicken stock

300ml full fat milk

salt and freshly ground black pepper

To serve

soured cream

chives, snipped

1.   Melt the butter in a large heavy-based saucepan. Add the leeks and onions and sweat – using a cartouche – for 30 minutes until the vegetables are soft but not coloured.

2.   Meanwhile peel and dice the potatoes – add them to the leeks and onions and add enough stock to cover the potatoes. Season with salt and pepper. Bring up to the boil and simmer for 15 minutes or until the potatoes are soft. Add the remaining stock and half of the milk.

3.   Whizz the soup in a blender until very smooth and then pass through a sieve. Add enough milk to bring the soup to the consistency of single cream. Season to taste.

4.   Chill or re-heat as required and swirl through the soured cream and sprinkle with the chives.

Stuffed Red Peppers

4 red peppers, halved lengthways, cored and seeded

olive oil

1 courgette, diced

100g couscous

85g sunblush tomatoes

grated zest of 1 lemon

125g mozzarella, cubed

3 tablespoons fresh basil, roughly chopped

4 small pieces anchovy

To garnish

small sprig of Greek basil

1. Preheat the grill to a high setting. Brush the peppers lightly with oil and grill, cut side down for 25 minutes or until just beginning to soften.

2. Fry the courgette in a little olive oil until just soft. Prepare the couscous according to the manufacturer's instructions.

3. Mix together the couscous, courgette, tomatoes, lemon zest and half of the mozzarella and basil. Season to taste.

4. Place a piece of anchovy in the bottom of each pepper half and fill with the couscous mixture.

5. Put a slice of mozzarella on top of each pepper and grill until lightly browned.

6. Serve on a plate garnished with a little basil.

Main Courses

Rack of Lamb with Mustard and Breadcrumbs

Most racks (also known as best end of lamb) are sold ready 'chined'. However, if buying from a buther do ask them to cut through the chine bone for you, otherwise it will be difficult to carve.

2 racks lamb, chined, trimmed and skinned

70g unsalted butter, softened

5 tablespoon fresh white breadcrumbs

2 tablespoons Dijon mustard

4 tablespoons chopped mixed fresh herbs such as mint, chives, parsley and rosemary*

salt and freshly ground black pepper

1.   Preheat the oven to 220C/425F, gas mark 7.

2.   Trim off all the fat you can from the racks of lamb and scrape the bones clean.

3.   Beat the butter until soft and add the breadcrumbs, mustard, herbs and salt and pepper.

4.   Spread a layer of this mixture neatly over the rounded skinned side of the best ends (racks). Put into a roasting tin (crumbed side up).

5.   Chill for at least 10 minutes. At this point the racks can be left overnight and cooked the next day if preferred.

6.   Roast for 20 minutes for pink lamb. Turn off the oven and leave to rest in the turned-off oven for 10 minutes.

*If using rosemary it must be very finely chopped.

Roasted Chicken with Clementines and Pernod

8 chicken thighs, trimmed of excess fat

100ml Pernod

60ml extra-virgin olive oil

3 tablespoons orange juice

3 tablespoons lemon juice

2 tablespoons wholegrain mustard

3 tablespoons light brown sugar

salt and freshly ground black pepper

2 medium fennel bulbs, trimmed

4 clementines, unpeeled and finely sliced horizontally

1 tablespoon fresh thyme leaves

2 teaspoons fennel seeds, lightly crushed

1. In a large mixing bowl, whisk the Pernod with the olive oil, orange juice, lemon juice, mustard and brown sugar. Whisk in the salt and black pepper and set aside.

2. Halve the fennel lengthwise and cut each half into 4 wedges. Add the fennel, chicken, clementines, thyme and fennel seeds to the bowl. Stir well with your hands, then cover with plastic wrap and refrigerate until you are ready to cook the chicken.

3. Preheat the oven to 220C/425F, gas mark 7. Transfer the chicken, fennel, clementines and marinade to a roasting pan large enough to accommodate everything in a single layer; the chicken skin should be facing up. Roast the chicken for 50–60 minutes or until it is browned and cooked through. Remove from the oven and transfer the chicken, fennel and clementines to a serving plate. Keep warm.

4. Pour the cooking liquid into a small saucepan set over medium-high heat. Bring the mixture to a boil, then simmer until the sauce is reduced; this may take up to 8 minutes. Pour the sauce over the chicken and serve immediately.

This is adapted from a recipe by Yotam Ottolenghi.

Chicken Salad with Beetroot and Feta Cheese and Salted Caramel Pecans

For salad

1 x 1.5kgs cooked chicken

2 large beetroot, cooked

1 pack feta cheese

200g sugar snap peas

4 tablespoons chives, freshly chopped

salt and ground black pepper

For the pecans

3 tablespoons granulated sugar

2 tablespoons water

15g unsalted butter

1 scant teaspoon salt

100g pecan halves

For the dressing

4 tablespoons olive oil

1 tablespoon balsamic vinegar

salt and freshly ground black pepper

1. Skin the chicken and break the flesh into even-sized pieces – discard all the bones and any gristle.

2. Prepare the pecans. Put the sugar, water, butter and salt into a heavy frying pan – heat gently until the sugar is almost dissolved – increase the heat and cook until just beginning to caramelise. Add the pecans and stir – using a metal fork – until well coated with dark caramel. This will take 2 to 3 minutes – be careful not to let the pan smoke. Tip onto a piece of parchment paper or 'Bake-O-Glide' paper and separate the pecans with 2 forks. Leave to cool but do not refrigerate.

3. Cut the beetroot and feta into similar sized cubes.

4. Blanch and refresh the sugar snaps.

5. Make the dressing by mixing the ingredients together – season with salt and pepper.

6. Place the chicken, beetroot, feta and sugar snaps in a bowl, together with three-quarters of the chives (keep the remainder to garnish with when you serve the salad).

Add the dressing and mix gently together. Pile into a serving dish.

7.   Scatter over the chives and salted pecans.

Note: To clean the pan and forks half fill the pan with water – submerge the forks and bring up to the boil – simmer for a couple of minutes by which time all the now-hard caramel should have dissolved.

Slow-Cooked Spiced Shanks of Lamb

4 lamb shanks

3 tablespoons sunflower oil

2 red onions, finely sliced

2 cloves garlic, crushed

1 2.5cm piece root ginger, peeled and grated

2 red chillies, finely chopped

2 tablespoons roasted spice mix (See page 155) or ras-el-hanout

2 x 400g chopped tomatoes

200ml red wine

2 teaspoons muscovado sugar

juice of 2 limes

1 small bunch coriander, leaves and stalks separated

1 bay leaf

salt and freshly ground black pepper

For the garnish

coriander leaves, roughly chopped (see above)

1.   Pre-heat the oven to 140C/275F, gas mark 1.

2.   Heat the oil in a large oven-proof, flame-proof casserole dish, add the lamb shanks and brown well all over.

3.   Remove the lamb to a plate and add the onions to the pan – you may need a little extra oil. Cook slowly until the onions are beginning to soften. Add the garlic, ginger, chillies, spice mix and tomatoes. Bring up to the boil stirring well.

4.   Add the wine, sugar, lime juice, coriander stalks and bay leaf. Return the lamb to the casserole dish and bring slowly up to the boil. Season well with salt and pepper, cover and place in the oven for 4 hours.

5.   Remove from the oven. Lift the lamb carefully from the pan, shaking off all the juices, and place on a warming serving dish. Cover with foil or wet greaseproof paper and return to the turned-off oven.

6.   Remove the bay leaf from the pan and skim off any fat. Re-heat the sauce. Taste and season as required.

7.   Spoon the sauce over the lamb shanks and scatter over very roughly chopped coriander.

Duck Breasts with Soured Cherry Sauce

4 duck breasts, with skin on

salt

oil

For the sauce

1 tablespoon oil

1 red onion, finely chopped

1 tablespoon soft brown sugar

2 tablespoons balsamic vinegar

150ml red wine

finely grated zest of 1 lime

60g dried soured cherries

To garnish

sprig of watercress

1. Pre-heat the oven to 200C/400F, gas mark 6.

2. Score the duck skin in fine diagonal lines. Rub salt and a little oil onto the skin.

3. Make the sauce: heat the oil in a small saucepan, add the onion and sweat slowly until soft. Add the sugar, increase the heat and cook until the sugar begins to caramelise. Carefully add the vinegar – it may sizzle a little, and then add the red wine, grated zest and cherries. Bring up to the boil and simmer for 5 minutes.

4. Place the duck, skin-side down, in a cold frying pan. Fry until lightly browned. Reduce the heat and continue to cook the duck slowly for about 10 minutes or until most of the fat has rendered down. Turn the breasts over and place skin-side up on a wire rack over a roasting pan. Bake for 8–10 minutes or until just firm. Turn off the oven and leave to rest for at least 5 minutes.

5. Remove the duck breasts from the oven, slice and place on a serving dish. Hand the sauce separately.

Note: The duck breasts can be fried a little in advance but do not refrigerate them.

Roasted Pork Belly with Orange and Star Anise

This recipe takes 8 hours to cook and it calls for white wine – this is not to enhance the flavour but simply to help tenderise the meat whilst it cooks at a very low temperature.

4 oranges, halved

2 tablespoons freshly chopped thyme

2 tablespoons freshly chopped rosemary

1 whole head garlic, cloves peeled and crushed

80ml olive oil

2 x 500g pieces pork belly, rind on and scored

oil

coarse sea salt and black pepper

400ml white wine

For the star anise reduction

250ml orange juice

90ml balsamic vinegar

80g honey

5 star anise

1. Preheat the oven to the highest temperature.

2. Arrange the orange halves in a large roasting tray, cut side up.

3. Put the herbs, garlic and oil in the small bowl of a food processor and whizz briefly.

4. Lay the scored pork on top of the orange halves, skin-side down, and spread the herb mixture evenly all over the upward-facing side of the meat, pressing so it sticks. Turn the joint over, so it is now skin-side up and sitting on the orange halves.

5. Rub a little oil over the pork and sprinkle with sea salt. Roast for 20 minutes or until the crackling is just beginning to brown and crisp. Reduce the oven to 140C/275F, gas mark 1. Remove the tin from the oven.

6. Push the oranges away from underneath the pork and then carefully pour in enough wine to come up to just below the rind – do not pour the wine

over the skin. Place the pan over a direct heat and bring the wine up to the boil and then place the pan immediately into the oven.

7. Roast for 8 hours. Meanwhile, prepare the sauce: put all the ingredients into a heavy-based pan, stir and place over a medium heat. Bring to the boil, reduce the heat and simmer for 45–60 minutes, until the sauce has reduced by half its original quantity. Remove from the heat and warm.

8. Remove the pork from the oven.

9. The crackling will not yet be crisp so remove it in one piece and place it under a hot grill and grill until crisp. (If the crackling is not easy to remove place the whole joint under the grill.) Watch it carefully – it can burn quite quickly.

10. Slice the meat and crackling as best you can and place on a serving dish. Serve garnished with a few of the orange halves.

11. Hand the sauce separately.

This is adapted from a recipe by Yotam Ottolenghi.

Hamburgers

400g rump steak, trimmed of all fat and cubed

400g sirloin, trimmed of all fat and cubed

salt and freshly ground black pepper

oil

To serve

4 baps

1. Put half the cubed rump in a food processor, pulse the blade 10 times, repeat for the other half of the rump. Do the same again for the sirloin. This is your mince.

2. Mix the mince in a large bowl, add the salt and pepper. Form into 4 hamburgers – do not over-work the meat.

3. Heat a lightly oiled cast iron griddle pan on medium high heat for 2–3 minutes. Cook the hamburgers for 4 minutes on each side for medium rare burgers. Flip the burgers only once. Serve in warm baps.

Roast Chicken

1 x 1.5kg chicken

½ lemon

½ apple

1 sprig rosemary

butter

½ bottle red wine

1 tablespoon redcurrant jelly

lemon juice

coarse sea salt and freshly ground black pepper

To serve

12 cocktail sausages

12 bacon rolls

bread sauce (see page 87)

1. Preheat the oven to 200C/400F, gas mark 6.

2. Clean the chicken and place the lemon, apple and rosemary inside the body cavity.

3. Carefully try to separate the breast skin from the flesh and push a little butter in the space on both sides of the breast. Smear a little butter over the breast of the chicken and place the chicken, breast side down, in a roasting tin. Season with salt and pepper and place in the oven. Roast for 40 minutes.

4. Put the sausages and bacon rolls into a small roasting tin and put them into the oven.

5. Remove the chicken from the oven and very carefully turn it over making sure that you don't break the skin on the breast. Pour the wine over the chicken, smear over a little more butter and return to the oven for a further 40 minutes or until the chicken is cooked. The juices will come out clear when the thigh is pierced with a skewer and the leg bones wobble independently from the body.

6. Remove the bacon rolls and sausages from the oven and keep warm.

7. Remove the cooked chicken, shaking any juices back into the roasting tin, to a warmed serving dish and cover with foil and keep warm while you make the gravy.

8. Carefully skim as much fat as possible from the meat juices and tip into a saucepan. Bring up to the boil; add half of the redcurrant jelly and a good squeeze of lemon juice. Season with salt and pepper. Simmer for 4–5 minutes. Taste the gravy and add more redcurrant jelly and lemon juice as required and season to taste.

9.   Joint the chicken (see page 159) and serve with the sausages, bacon and bread sauce.

Chilli con Carne

1 tablespoon oil

400g lean minced beef

1 onion, finely chopped

1 large clove garlic, crushed

2 teaspoons hot chilli powder

1 teaspoon ground cumin

2 x 400g cans chopped tomatoes

1 x 400g can kidney beans, rinsed and drained

1 teaspoon muscovado sugar

5g dark cooking chocolate (such as Green and Black)

salt and freshly ground black pepper

To serve

soured cream

tortilla chips

To garnish

leaves of coriander

1.   Heat a large frying pan and add the oil. Add the mince and brown it well. Use a fork to break it up and add the onion. The mince should become brown all over and there should be no lumps. Add the garlic, chilli and cumin and cook for a further minute.

2.   Tip into a saucepan. Add the tomatoes. Rinse out the cans and add the water from the cans to the mince. Season with salt and pepper and place the pan over the heat. Bring up to the boil and allow to simmer, stirring occasionally.

3.   After 1 hour add the beans, sugar and chocolate, stir very well and return to the heat for a further hour, stirring occasionally or until the mince is tender and the juices are syrupy. If it gets too thick add a little water. If it seems too runny boil vigorously until syrupy.

4.   Serve in bowls with the soured cream and tortilla chips and garnish with the coriander leaves.

Paella

Recipes for paella are legion but this one, very slightly adapted from a recipe by Simon Hopkinson, is my favourite. It is essential to use paella rice such as Calasparra.

150ml dry sherry

250g cherry tomatoes, halved

4 cloves garlic, peeled and chopped

1 teaspoon smoked Spanish paprika

2 tablespoons olive oil

200g chorizo sausage, skinned and cut into small chunks

1 medium squid, cleaned and cut into rings

4 boneless chicken thighs, trimmed and cut in half

100g runner beans, stringed and sliced

150g sweet red peppers from a jar, sliced

1 teaspoon saffron threads soaked in 2 tablespoons hot water

800ml chicken stock, hot

300g paella rice

500g mussels, cleaned and de-bearded

salt and freshly ground black pepper

To finish

3 cloves garlic, finely chopped

2 tablespoons freshly chopped curly parsley

4 tablespoons olive oil

lemon wedges

1. Liquidise together the sherry, tomatoes, garlic and paprika.

2. Heat the oil in a paella pan, add the chorizo and fry until the fat begins to run – remove with a slotted spoon to a plate. Add the squid and fry briefly. Remove to the same plate.

3. Brown the chicken in the same pan until just brown.

4. Add the sherry mixture to the pan with the chicken and bring up to a simmer. Cook for 5 minutes.

5. Add the beans, peppers and saffron 'tea'.

6. Add the chorizo and squid and pour in the stock. Stir well and bring up to a simmer.

7. Sprinkle the rice evenly into the pan. The paella should not be stirred once the rice has been added – the rice will stick a little at the bottom of the pan but is delicious – it is called socorat.

8. Season the paella with salt and freshly ground black pepper and cook over a medium heat – the rice can take anything from 12 to 25 minutes to cook so taste it every so often to see.

9. Preheat the oven to 180C/350F, gas mark 4.

10. Prepare the finish – mix the garlic, parsley and oil together.

11. When the rice is just cooked press the mussels, hinged side down, into the rice. Cover with tin foil and bake in the oven for 5 minutes or until all the mussels have opened.

12. Drizzle the garlic, parsley and oil mixture over the paella and serve with lemon wedges.

Notes: Before cooking with mussels be sure that they are alive – tap any that are open and if they don't close they should be discarded – also discard any that feel heavy compared to the other mussels.

If preferred the mussels can be steamed separately and then added to the paella just before serving.

The amount of liquid called for is a little by and large as it depends on the size of your pan and the heat at which the paella is cooked – if you need extra liquid simply add some hot water.

Spaghetti Bolognaise

400g spaghetti

For the sauce

1 tablespoon oil

400g lean minced beef

1 small onion, finely chopped

1 stick celery, finely chopped

I small carrot, peeled and finely chopped

1 large clove garlic, crushed

100g flat mushrooms, chopped

100ml red wine

300ml brown stock

1 x 400g can chopped tomatoes or jar of passata

salt and freshly ground black pepper

2 tablespoons full fat milk

To serve

olive oil

shavings of fresh Parmesan cheese

1. Heat a large frying pan and add the oil. Add the mince and brown it well. Use a fork to break it up and add the onion, celery and carrot. The mince should become brown all over and there should be no lumps. Add the garlic and mushrooms and cook for a further minute.

2. Tip into a saucepan. Pour the red wine into the frying pan and bring to the boil, scraping the bottom of the pan with a wooden spoon to loosen all the sediment. Add to the mince with the stock. Add the tomatoes. Rinse out the can or bottle and add the water to the mince. Season with salt and pepper and place over the heat. Bring up to the boil and allow to simmer, stirring occasionally, for 2 hours until the mince is tender and the juices are syrupy. If it gets too thick add a little water. If it seems too runny boil vigorously until syrupy. Just before you are ready to serve add the milk and boil briefly, stirring continually. The milk absorbs any fat and gives the Bolognaise sauce a rich creamy finish.

3. While the sauce is cooking push the spaghetti into a large saucepan of boiling salted water to which a tablespoon of oil has been added. Boil until just tender and drain in a large colander. Rinse with a kettleful of boiling water and pile into a serving dish. Toss through two tablespoons of olive oil and serve with the Bolognaise sauce and the shavings of Parmesan cheese.

Meatballs with Orzo

For the meatballs

500g lean minced beef

500g lean minced pork

1 red onion, very finely chopped

2 tablespoons fresh flat-leaf parsley (or parlsey and coriander), finely chopped

180g Philadelphia cheese

1 tablespoon roasted spice mix (see page 155) or ras-el-hanout

grated zest of 2 lemons

salt and freshly ground black pepper

oil for frying

tomato sauce (see page 95) (note it is not necessary to liquidise the sauce)

To serve

600g orzo

To garnish

basil, freshly chopped

1.   Put all the ingredients for the meatballs into a bowl and using your hands mix well. Season with salt and pepper.

2.   With wet hands shape, kneading the mixture well as you shape, into meatballs of an even size.

3.   Heat a large non-stick frying pan. Add a drop of sunflower oil, and quickly brown meatballs all over in batches.

4.   Preheat the oven to 180C/350F, gas mark 4.

5.   Pour half of the tomato sauce into the base of a large lidded oven-proof dish. Then carefully arrange the meatballs on top of the sauce and cover with remaining sauce – place over the direct heat and bring the sauce to the boil. Remove from the heat and cover the pan.

6.   Place the meatballs in the oven for about 40 minutes, or until the meatballs are cooked.

7.   Cook the orzo in boiling salted water, to which a tablespoon of oil has been added, according to the manufacturer's instructions.

8.   Pile the meatballs into a dish and serve garnished with basil.

9.   Hand the orzo separately.

Serves 6

Roast Leg of Lamb with Rosemary

Serves 6

1 leg of lamb, about 2kg

3 large rosemary sprigs

2 cloves garlic, peeled and thinly sliced

4 anchovy fillets, cut in half

300ml red wine

salt and freshly ground black pepper

For the gravy

1 teaspoon redcurrant jelly

tomato puree

Worcester sauce

balsamic vinegar

1. Heat the oven to 220C/425F, gas mark 7.

2. Weigh the lamb and calculate the cooking time as 45 minutes per kilo plus 20 minutes (for pink in the middle), allowing for more or less time according to how you like your lamb cooked.

3. Season the lamb well with salt and pepper. Make about 8 small incisions into the flesh and insert half an anchovy fillet and a sliver of garlic into each incision. Place in a roasting tin, just big enough to accommodate the meat, tuck the rosemary sprigs underneath and roast in the oven for 20 minutes, then lower the oven setting to 190C/375F, gas mark 5. After 45 minutes' roasting, pour the wine over the lamb.

4. Check the meat 30 minutes before the end of the cooking time; depending on the joint, the lamb may be done a little earlier than the calculated time. Insert a skewer through the thickest part for 10 seconds. Remove the skewer and check the heat against your inner wrist; it should be warm.

5. Once the lamb is cooked, transfer it to a board over a tray to catch the juices and leave to rest for at least 15–20 minutes while you make the gravy.

6. Pour off the fat and juices from the roasting tin into a bowl and allow them to separate; adding a splash of cold water helps this.

7. Return the juices to the roasting tin. Add the redcurrant jelly and bring to a simmer. Simmer for 2–3 minutes, then season to taste with salt and pepper. Add any juices released from the meat while it is resting to the gravy. Taste and season as required; you may like to add tomato puree, balsamic vinegar or Worcester sauce.

8. Carve the lamb and serve the gravy separately.

Note: You can roast shoulder of lamb in the same way.

Fillet of Beef with Salsa Verde

1 x 600g piece beef fillet – taken from the thick end

olive oil

1 tablespoon black peppercorns, crushed

½ tablespoon sea salt

1. Pre-heat the oven to 220C/425F, gas mark 7.

2. Rub the beef in a little olive oil.

3. Crush the peppercorns and salt together and roll the beef in the seasoning – press down firmly so that it sticks to the meat.

4. Heat a little oil in a roasting pan and when beginning to sizzle add the beef and brown evenly all over. Place the pan in the oven and roast for 12 minutes. Remove from the oven and leave to cool.

5. When cold slice finely and serve with salsa verde (page 94).

Roast Chicken with Mustard and Lemon

8 chicken thighs, trimmed of excess fat

30g butter, softened

2 tablespoons Dijon mustard

1 teaspoon caster sugar

1 teaspoon paprika

juice of ½ lemon

salt and freshly ground black pepper

1.   Preheat the oven to 200C/400F, gas mark 6.

2.   Mix together the butter, mustard, sugar, paprika and lemon juice.
        Don't worry if the mixture looks a little curdled.

3.   Spread the mixture over the chicken thighs, season with salt and pepper and
        place in the oven for one hour, basting the chicken once or twice.

4.   Remove from the oven and place the chicken on a serving dish.

5.   Tip the cooking juices into a small saucepan and boil rapidly until the sauce
        reduces and begins to emulsify. Pour over the chicken.

Miso Cod

This recipe is best prepared a day in advance.

4 x 170g pieces of cod loin, pin boned and skinned

150ml mirrin

150ml sake

4 tablespoons pale miso paste

2 tablespoons granulated sugar

For the garnish

fresh coriander

To serve

pickled ginger and wasabi

1.   Place the mirrin, sake, miso paste and sugar in a saucepan, bring gradually to the boil and then simmer until the sugar has dissolved. Pour over the cod and leave to marinade for up to 24 hours.

2.   Preheat the grill.

3.   Place the cod on a grill pan lined with aluminium foil. Grill for 2–3 minutes. Pile onto a plate; tip all the juices into a small saucepan and boil rapidly until syrupy. Spoon over the fish, garnish with coriander.

4.   Serve with pickled ginger and wasabi.

Note: There is a large variety of miso pastes available – buy the best quality that you can find.

Baked Salmon with Roasted New Potatoes

Lightly smoked salmon fillets are available in most good supermarkets.

4 lightly smoked salmon fillets

oil for frying

flour

500g new potatoes

8 whole shallots, peeled

4 cloves garlic, unpeeled

olive oil

2 sprigs rosemary

rock salt and freshly ground black pepper

To serve

chilli sauce (see page 92)

To garnish

1 sprig rosemary

1.   Preheat the oven to 200C/400F, gas mark 6.

2.   Dust the salmon fillets lightly with flour and sprinkle with salt. Fry until very slightly browned in the oil. Set aside.

3.   Meanwhile put the potatoes into a roasting pan with the shallots and garlic and turn them in the olive oil. Add the rosemary and season with salt and pepper. Bake for 20 minutes.

4.   Remove from the oven and add the salmon fillets to the pan. Make sure that the fillets are kept as flat as possible.

5.   Bake for a further 10 minutes and remove from the oven. Discard the cooked rosemary and garnish the salmon with the fresh rosemary. Serve from the pan and hand the chilli sauce separately.

Goujons of Sole

See safety notes on deep-fat frying: page 161.

dry breadcrumbs

½ teaspoon cayenne pepper

2 lemon sole, skinned and filleted

sunflower oil, for frying

plain flour

beaten egg

2 lemons, cut into wedges

1. Mix the breadcrumbs with the cayenne pepper and set aside.

2. Cut each lemon sole or sole fillets into strips on the diagonal about 1cm/½in thick.

3. Heat the oil in a deep-fat fryer to 190C/375F.

4. Coat the fish in flour, then the beaten egg and finally the crumbs; a few pieces at a time, making sure all the fish is coated thoroughly. Shake off any excess flour, egg or crumbs at each stage. The goujons should be kept on a plate but keep them separate so that they do not go soggy.

5. Place a few of the goujons in the fryer at a time and cook for about one minute, until crisp and golden brown. Repeat until all the goujons are cooked.

6. Once cooked, remove onto some kitchen paper to soak up the excess oil.

Note: Most standard domestic fryers need just over 2 litres of oil to be filled to the correct level.

Salmon Burgers with Red Onion, Caper and Parsley Salad

Serves 6

1kg salmon, skinned and pin boned

1 x 2.5cm piece ginger, peeled and grated

3 garlic cloves, peeled and finely chopped

2 chillies, seeded and finely chopped

½ bunch coriander, chopped

juice and finely grated zest of 1 lemon

salt and freshly ground black pepper

For the salad

1 red onion, finely sliced

small handful of capers, well rinsed

1 bunch of parsley, roughly chopped

French dressing (see page 90)

To serve

6 burger buns

mayonnaise (see page 89)

baby gem lettuce, shredded

1. Finely chop the salmon.

2. Mix all the remaining ingredients for the burger together with the salmon. Season with salt and pepper.

3. Make the salad – mix all the ingredients together with the French dressing.

4. Using wet hands shape the salmon mixture into six equal-sized burgers, then sear the burgers in a hot, lightly oiled griddle or frying pan for about 2 minutes on each side.

5. Place between a burger bun with a little mayonnaise and the shredded lettuce, serve with the salad.

This is adapted from a recipe by Sam Harrison.

Miso Salmon with Black Rice

Lightly smoked salmon fillets are available in most good supermarkets.

4 lightly smoked salmon fillets

5 tablespoons sweet white miso paste

mirrin

150g black rice

sesame oil

200g French beans, trimmed and cut into short pieces

For the dressing

3 tablespoons sweet white miso paste

4 tablespoons yuzu

To serve

1 small punnet mixed cherry tomatoes, halved

fresh dill

1. Preheat the oven to 200C/400F, gas mark 6. Set the grill to the highest setting.

2. Cook the rice according to the manufacturer's instructions – it will take between 30 and 45 minutes.

3. Place the salmon, skin-side down, on a baking sheet lined with a lightly oiled piece of Bakewell paper or some 'Bake-O-Glide'.

4. Mix the miso to a 'sludgy paste' with the mirin and spoon evenly over the salmon.

5. Bake for 8 minutes and then place under the grill until evenly browned.

6. Cook the beans in salted boiling water until al dente.

7. Make the dressing – mix the ingredients together and season to taste. If it is too thick add a little water or a splash of orange juice.

8. Put the rice and beans into a bowl and very gently mix them together, then add the dressing. Stir gently to mix. Pile down the length of a serving dish or onto individual plates and arrange the salmon over the rice. Scatter over the tomatoes. Garnish with the dill.

Note: If you can't get hold of any yuzu use 2 tablespoons each of fresh orange and lemon juice. Sesame oil goes off pretty quickly so check the use-by date.

Fish Pie

600g haddock or cod fillet, pin boned

500ml milk

½ onion, sliced

6 black peppercorns

1 bay leaf

1 tablespoon freshly chopped parsley

3 hard-boiled eggs (see page 153) peeled and quartered

150g cooked prawns

50g butter

50g flour

salt and freshly ground black pepper

mashed potatoes (see page 83)

To finish

butter

grated Cheddar cheese, optional

1. Preheat the oven to 180C/350F, gas mark 4.

2. Lay the fish fillets in a roasting tin skin-side up. Heat half of the milk and pour it over the fish. Add the onion, peppercorns, bay leaf and a pinch of salt. Cover with a piece of crumpled, damp greaseproof paper and place in the oven for 15 minutes or until the fish is cooked. The flesh should feel firm, look opaque and the skin should pull off easily. Remove the fish to a board and strain the milk into a measuring jug – make it up to 500ml with the remaining milk.

3. Skin the fish and flake into large pieces – place in a pie dish and cover.

4. Meanwhile make the sauce: melt the butter in a small saucepan, add the flour and cook for one minute. Remove from the heat and gradually add the milk, stirring continuously trying to avoid getting any lumps (but don't worry if you do – a sauce whisk can come to the rescue later). When you have added about a quarter of the milk return the pan to the heat and add the remaining milk, stirring continuously as you bring the sauce to the boil. Simmer for at least two minutes – if there are any lumps whisk vigorously with a sauce whisk. Add the parsley and season to taste.

5. Add the hard-boiled eggs and prawns to the fish and then pour over the sauce and very carefully mix it together – you do not want to break the fish up.

6.   Preheat the grill.

7.   Spread a layer of mashed potatoes on top of the pie and mark it with a fork or pipe the potatoes on top of the pie. Dot with a little butter and scatter over the grated cheese, if using.

8.   Place on a baking sheet and bake in the oven for about 30 minutes or until the pie is hot. To test, insert a skewer into the centre of the pie and then very carefully place the skewer on the inside of your wrist – if it is hot you will be able to feel the heat before you actually have to touch your skin.

9.   Place under the hot grill to brown the top.

Grilled Sea Bass with Salmoriglio Sauce

4 x 170g sea bass fillets, pin boned

1 tablespoon olive oil

salt and freshly ground black pepper

For the sauce

100ml extra-virgin olive oil

½ shallot, finely chopped

2 cloves garlic, crushed

2 tablespoons freshly chopped parsley

1 tablespoon freshly chopped oregano

juice of 1 lemon

1.   Heat the grill to its highest setting.

2.   Heat the oil in a small saucepan, add the shallot and sweat for 5 minutes. Add the garlic and leave over the heat for a further minute.

3.   Remove from the heat and add the herbs – add lemon juice to taste (saving a little for the fish). Season with salt and pepper.

4.   Brush the skin-side of the sea bass with the oil, place skin-side up (the fish cooks without overcooking and the skin gets crisp) upon a lightly oiled baking sheet and season with salt, pepper and lemon juice. Grill for 4 minutes.

5.   Transfer to a warm plate and spoon over some of the sauce to serve. Hand the rest separately.

This recipe has been taken from *How to Cook* by Leiths School of Food and Wine.

Wild Mushroom Risotto

30g butter

1 onion, finely chopped

1 clove of garlic, crushed

30g dried porcini, soaked in 150ml boiling water for 15 minutes

200g wild mushrooms, brushed clean and sliced

175g risotto rice

250ml dry white wine

600ml vegetable stock, hot

salt and freshly ground black pepper

To finish

20g unsalted butter

50g Parmesan cheese, freshly grated

1.   Melt the butter in a large sauté pan and cook the onion slowly until soft but not coloured.

2.   Drain the porcini, strain the soaking liquid and add it to the hot stock. Rinse the porcini.

3.   Add the risotto rice to the onions and cook until glassy. Add the garlic and mushrooms and sauté for a further 1–2 minutes.

4.   Add the wine and stir well – cook until the wine is absorbed.

5.   Start adding the hot stock, with the porcini liquid, to the rice a little at a time, stirring very gently. Allow the stock to become absorbed after each addition – continue until all the stock has been used and the rice is al dente. The sauce should become very creamy. The amount of stock required may vary but if you run out top it up using boiling water.

6.   Remove the pan from the heat and add the butter and Parmesan cheese and mix gently until the butter is melted and the cheese absorbed. Allow the risotto to stand for 5 minutes before serving.

Macaroni Cheese

For the sauce

20g butter

scant 20g flour

pinch English mustard powder

pinch cayenne pepper

350ml milk

100g strong Cheddar cheese, grated

salt and freshly ground black pepper

For the pasta

150g macaroni

To finish

dried white breadcrumbs

1. Cook the macaroni in plenty of boiling salted water until just tender (al dente). Drain the macaroni well and rinse with boiling water.

2. Meanwhile make the cheese sauce. Melt the butter in a small pan, add the flour, mustard and cayenne and cook, stirring with a wooden spoon, over a gentle heat for 1 minute.

3. Remove from the heat and very gradually add the milk – stir well between each addition and make sure that it is well incorporated before adding more. When about half of the milk has been added you can add the remaining milk more quickly – stirring well all the time.

4. Return the pan to a moderate heat and, stirring well, bring the milk to the boil. The sauce should gradually thicken. Once thickened allow the sauce to simmer for 2 minutes. Remove from the heat and add all but 2 tablespoons of the cheese.

5. Set the grill to its highest setting.

6. Season the sauce to taste. Add the drained macaroni to the sauce and stir well.

7. Transfer the mixture to a heat-proof dish and scatter over the reserved cheese and breadcrumbs.

8. Place under the grill until golden brown and serve.

Note: If preparing this in advance, assemble the dish as in the recipe but use 130g rather than 150g of macaroni and then bake in a preheated oven (200C/400F, gas mark 6) for 30 minutes and then scatter over the cheese and breadcrumbs and grill as before.

Roast Vegetables with Pine Nuts and Feta Cheese

2 aubergines cut into 3cm cubes

2 courgettes cut into 3cm cubes

4 red onions, peeled and quartered

2 tablespoons olive oil

2 Romano peppers, halved lengthways and seeded

2 tablespoons basil, freshly chopped

1 punnet baby plum tomatoes, halved

1 x 200g packet feta cheese, cubed

40g pine nuts

1 tablespoon balsamic vinegar (optional)

salt and freshly ground black pepper

1.   Preheat the oven to 200C/400F, gas mark 6.

2.   Put the aubergines, courgettes and red onions into a large roasting tin. Drizzle with the olive oil and season with salt and pepper.

3.   Bake for 20 minutes. Remove from the oven and add the peppers, half the basil and the tomatoes, give the vegetables a gentle stir and then scatter over the feta cheese and pine nuts. Drizzle over the balsamic vinegar and return to the oven for 20 minutes or until the vegetables are tender and the cheese and nuts are lightly browned.

4.   Scatter over the remaining basil and serve.

Aubergine and Butternut Squash Salad

1 small butternut squash, peeled and cut into 2.5cm/1" cubes

1 large aubergine, cut into cubes a little larger than the squash

2 courgettes, thickly sliced

extra-virgin olive oil

To finish

2 pinches saffron threads

1 tablespoon boiling water

2 tablespoons plain yogurt

2 tablespoons pomegranate seeds

1 tablespoon pumpkin seeds

1 teaspoon nigella seeds

salt and freshly ground black pepper

1. Preheat the oven to 200C/400F, gas mark 6.

2. Put the squash into an oven-proof tray with the aubergine and courgettes. Drizzle with olive oil. Season with salt and pepper, stir to coat with the oil and bake for 30 minutes or until the vegetables are cooked.

3. Meanwhile prepare the dressing. Grind the saffron lightly, put into a small bowl and pour over the boiling water.

4. Leave to stand for 10 minutes.

5. Add the 'saffron tea' to the yogurt.

6. When the vegetables are cooked remove from the oven and pile onto a plate.

7. Whilst the vegetables are still warm drizzle the yogurt dressing over them and sprinkle with the pomegranate, pumpkin and nigella seeds.

This is adapted from a recipe by Tina Fraser.

Butternut Squash Pasta with Deep-Fried Sage

For the filling

800g butternut squash (prepared weight), peeled and seeded

1 red onion, chopped into chunks

2 tablespoons olive oil

salt and freshly ground black pepper

semolina

To serve

3 tablespoons olive oil

12 large sage leaves

shavings of fresh Parmesan cheese

extra olive oil

400g fresh pasta (page 152)

1. Preheat the oven to 200C/400F, gas mark 6.

2. Cut the butternut squash into equal-sized pieces and place in a roasting tin; add the onion. Drizzle with oil and season well with salt and pepper.

3. Place in the oven for 50 minutes or until the squash and onion are well cooked. Check them every so often and turn them in the pan to prevent burning. Remove from the oven and leave to cool slightly.

4. Put into a food processor and whizz until very smooth. Check the seasoning and set aside.

5. Roll out a piece of pasta (make sure the rest of the pasta is well wrapped in cling film) and lay it on a work surface dusted with semolina. Spoon the filling at intervals along the length of the pasta. Using a pastry brush, brush a little water around each mound of filling. Roll out a second sheet of pasta and carefully lay the pasta on top of the first sheet. Starting with the middle of the pasta, carefully seal and shape the ravioli with your fingers – try to make sure that there are no air bubbles left. Once all are covered, carefully cut out the ravioli using a floured pastry cutter. Transfer to a tray dusted with plenty of semolina.

6. Repeat the rolling and filling process until all the pasta and filling have been used. Make sure that the ravioli are placed on a surface, such as a tray, that has been dusted with semolina. Allow to dry for 15 minutes or so.

7. Meanwhile bring a large pan of salted water, to which a tablespoon of oil has been added, to the boil.

8. Heat the olive oil for the garnish and when very hot add the sage leaves and fry until they look almost translucent. Drain well on kitchen paper.

9. Cook the pasta for 2–3 minutes and then drain well and toss in olive oil. Pile into a warm serving dish and garnish with the deep-fried sage and hand the Parmesan cheese separately.

Note: If making this in advance it is very important that the tray is well dusted with semolina – it will all disappear when you cook the pasta. If you make it 24 hours in advance it is a good idea to check that the ravioli are not sticking to the tray after about 4 hours, and if they are dust a clean tray with semolina and carefully remove the pasta to the new tray. Do not cover the pasta (the cling film will stick to the pasta) and place in the fridge overnight.

Vegetables and Salads

Salt and Vinegar "Chips"

700g new potatoes, washed

olive oil

coarse sea salt and freshly ground black pepper

2 tablespoons balsamic vinegar

1. Set the oven to 200C/400F, gas mark 6.

2. Cut each potato into 6 wedges, lengthways, and put them into a roasting tin. Drizzle liberally with olive oil. Season with plenty of sea salt and black pepper.

3. Put the roasting tin into the top of the oven and cook for 50–60 minutes turning occasionally or until the potatoes are crisp and brown. Pour over the balsamic vinegar and toss the chips in it.

Pear and Fennel Salad with Pecorino

1 large fennel bulb, quartered, cored and sliced very finely

1 tablespoon lemon juice

3 tablespoons virgin olive oil

3 teaspoons maple syrup

2 conference pears, peeled, quartered and sliced

50g pecorino cheese, finely shaved

35g rocket

2 tablespoons freshly chopped dill

salt and freshly ground black pepper

1. Blanch the fennel in boiling salted water for 2 minutes. Drain and refresh under running cold water until completely cold. Pat dry with kitchen paper.

2. Mix together the lemon juice, oil and maple syrup. Add to the fennel. Taste and season well – the lemon can make the dressing taste a little sour so extra maple syrup may be necessary.

3. Add the conference pears and make sure they are coated in the dressing. Add half of the dill and mix well. Add the cheese and mix in gently.

4. Scatter the rocket over the base of a serving dish – pile on the salad and scatter over the remaining dill.

Puy Lentil and Pancetta Salad

200g puy lentils

10 rashers pancetta

1 clove garlic, lightly crushed

2 bay leaves

sprig of thyme

1 tablespoon oil

1 carrot, peeled and finely sliced

1 leek, finely sliced

1 shallot, finely chopped

1 glass dry white wine

2 tomatoes, peeled and diced

1 tablespoon freshly chopped parsley

4 spring onions, chopped

For the dressing

3 tablespoons olive oil

1 tablespoon balsamic vinegar

1 teaspoon grainy mustard

salt and freshly ground black pepper

1.   Preheat the oven to 200C/400F, gas mark 6.

2.   Place the pancetta rashers on a baking sheet and cook in the oven for 5–6 minutes or until nicely browned and crisp. Drain well on kitchen paper.

3.   Rinse the lentils well, place in a pan of cold water. Add the garlic, bay leaves and thyme. Cook according to the manufacturer's instructions until just tender. Drain well and leave to cool. Remove the garlic, bay leaves and thyme.

4.   Heat the oil in a small frying pan and add the carrot, leek and shallot and cook until just soft. Add the white wine and reduce, by boiling rapidly, to a glaze. Add to the lentils.

5.   Add the tomatoes, parsley and spring onions.

6.   Make the dressing – whisk all the ingredients together and stir into the lentil salad. Season to taste.

7.   Roughly chop the pancetta and mix into the lentil salad just before serving.

Roast New Potatoes with Leeks and Harissa

Serves 4

600g new potatoes, washed and halved

2 tablespoons harissa paste

½ teaspoon ground cumin

6 tablespoons olive oil

2 leeks, chopped (white part only)

finely grated zest of 1 lemon

salt and freshly ground black pepper

To serve

½ bunch dill, freshly chopped

plain yogurt flavoured with crushed garlic

1. Preheat the oven to 200C/400F, gas mark 6.

2. Mix together 4 tablespoons of the oil, the harissa and cumin in a bowl; add the potatoes – mix well. Season and place in a roasting tin and bake for 20 minutes.

3. Meanwhile mix the leeks with the remaining oil and the lemon zest. Pile on top of the potatoes – stir briefly and return to the oven for a further 20 minutes or until the potatoes are tender.

4. While the potatoes are cooking add the garlic to the yogurt.

5. Put the potatoes into a serving dish – scatter over the dill and hand the yogurt separately.

Kohlrabi and Beetroot Salad

1 large kohlrabi

2 dessert apples

2 large raw beetroot

3 tablespoons coriander, freshly chopped

1 clove garlic, crushed

25ml cider vinegar

75ml olive oil

salt and freshly ground black pepper

To serve

fresh coriander, roughly chopped

1. Peel the kohlrabi, cut in half and grate as finely as possible.

2. Peel and core the apples and grate finely.

3. Peel the beetroot and grate very finely. Mix the grated vegetables together.

4. Mix together the coriander, garlic, vinegar and oil. Add to the prepared vegetables and season well with salt and pepper.

5. Pile into a serving dish and scatter over the roughly chopped coriander.

Note: When kohlrabi is not in season use celeriac.

Giant Couscous Salad

For the rocket pesto

25g fresh basil leaves

25g fresh rocket

1–2 garlic cloves, peeled and roughly chopped

25g pine nuts

6 tablespoons extra-virgin olive oil

15g Parmesan cheese, freshly grated

salt and ground black pepper

lemon juice, to taste

For the couscous salad

200g giant couscous

80g buffalo mozzarella roughly chopped

80g chorizo, skinned and sliced, grilled or fried

25g rocket

10g toasted pine nuts

salt and freshly ground black pepper

1. Cook the couscous: tip it into a pan of boiling stock and boil for 6–8 minutes, stirring occasionally. Drain using a sieve and leave to cool.

2. Meanwhile, make pesto by food processing the basil, rocket, cheese, garlic, pine nuts and 2 tablespoons of the olive oil; process to a fairly smooth paste. Gradually add the remaining oil and season with salt and pepper.

3. Once the couscous is cool, combine with the pesto and half the rocket, and toss thoroughly.

4. Just before serving add the remaining ingredients including the rocket, and season to taste.

Fatoush

2 small gem lettuces

2 pitta or 1 flatbread

1 tablespoon oil

1 cucumber, peeled, seeded and diced

½ red onion, finely chopped

1 tablespoon black olives, pitted

1 x 200g packet feta cheese, crumbled

2 tablespoons pomegranate seeds

150g cherry tomatoes, halved

150g radishes, trimmed and quartered

For the dressing

3 tablespoons olive oil

1 tablespoon lemon juice

1 tablespoon balsamic vinegar

salt and freshly ground black pepper

To serve

1 tablespoon sumac

2 tablespoons Greek yogurt

1.   Wash and dry the lettuces and cut into wedges.

2.   Cut the pitta bread into quarters and fry in the oil until lightly crisped. Drain well on kitchen paper. If using flatbread fry it for a minute on each side and then cut into smallish pieces.

3.   Put the lettuces into a salad bowl with the cucumber, onion, olives, feta, pomegranate seeds, tomatoes and radishes.

4.   Mix the ingredients together for the dressing and toss into the salad. Add the fried bread and serve with the sumac and Greek yogurt mixed together.

Note: There are very many versions of Fatoush but the essential ingredients are sumac and lemon juice. If you find the dressing too sour add a little maple syrup.

Green Salad

1 lettuce (any kind)

French dressing (see page 90)

choice of the following:

cucumber

fennel

celery

chicory

spring onions

watercress

green beans

peas

1 teaspoon chopped fresh mint, parsley or chives

1. Prepare the salad ingredients.

    Lettuce: wash, drain and shake to dry. Do not twist or wring the leaves together, which bruises them, but tear each lettuce leaf individually into bite-sized pieces and place in a salad bowl.

    Cucumber: peel or not, as desired. Slice thinly.

    Fennel: wash and shave into thin slices. Blanch if preferred.

    Chicory: wipe with a damp cloth. Remove the tough core with a sharp knife and cut each head on the diagonal into 3–4 pieces.

    Spring onions: wash and peel. Remove any tough stalks or dry outer leaves. Chop half the green stalks finely. Keep the white part with the rest of the salad.

    Watercress: wash and pick over, discarding the thick stalks and any yellow leaves.

    Beans and peas: cook in boiling salted water until just tender and cool under cold running water. Drain well and pat dry in a tea towel.

2. Add the herbs and the spring onion tops to the dressing.

3. Mix the salad ingredients together and just before serving toss them in French dressing.

Chips

See deep-fat frying notes on page 161.

675g potatoes (Maris Piper)

oil for deep-frying

salt

1. Cut the potatoes into 5cm x 1cm/2" x ½" sticks. Keep them in a bowl of cold water until ready for cooking. Dry them very well on kitchen paper and blanch in boiling salted water for 2 minutes. Drain well. The potatoes must be dry before they are deep fried.

2. Heat the oil in a deep-fryer to a medium temperature – when a crumb of bread is dropped in it should sizzle gently.

3. Dry the potatoes carefully and place a few at a time in the chip basket – too many will stick together.

4. Fry for 7–8 minutes until soft. Remove from the oil.

5. Heat the oil again, until a crumb of bread will sizzle and brown in just 20 seconds. The oil should be at 190C.

6. Repeat the frying process in the hotter oil until the chips are well browned and crisp.

7. Drain the chips on absorbent kitchen paper. Sprinkle with salt.

8. Serve immediately. Do not cover the chips or they will lose their crispness.

Note: Chips are cooked in three stages – the first (blanching) is to remove excess starch. The second (first frying) is because if the fat is hot enough to crisp and brown the chips, the middle of the potato will not be cooked. On the other hand, if the oil is cooler, although the chip will cook through, it will be soggy. The second frying (stage 3), to create the crisp brown outside, should be done just before serving.

Roast Potatoes

Serves 4

900g potatoes

salt

4 tablespoons dripping, oil or goose fat

1. Preheat the oven to 200C/400F, gas mark 6.

2. Wash and peel the potatoes and, if they are large, cut them into 5cm/2" pieces.

3. Bring them to the boil in salted water. Simmer for 10 minutes. Drain well, return to the pan and shake the potatoes to roughen their surfaces.

4. Melt the dripping, oil or goose fat in a roasting pan and when hot add the potatoes, turning them so that they are coated all over. Take care if using goose fat – it can spit and may burn you. Season with salt and pepper.

5. Roast, basting occasionally, and turning the potatoes over halfway through cooking.

Notes: Potatoes can be roasted at almost any temperature, usually taking 1 hour in a hot oven, or 1½ hours in a moderate one. They should be basted and turned over once or twice during cooking, and they are done when a skewer glides easily into them. Potatoes roasted in the same pan as meat have the best flavour, but will not be as crisp as potatoes roasted only in fat.

The potatoes can be prepared to the end of stage 4 a day in advance.

The water in which the potatoes were parboiled can be saved and used for making gravy if no stock is available.

Maris Piper potatoes are the best for roasting.

Mashed Potatoes

If using this recipe for a pie topping start with about 200ml milk and add more as required.

1kg floury potatoes (such as Maris Piper), peeled and cut to 5cm/2" pieces

salt and ground white pepper

250ml milk

60g butter

a little freshly grated nutmeg

1.   Put the potatoes into a saucepan of cold, salted water. Bring to the boil and simmer until tender. Drain thoroughly.

2.   Return them to the dry saucepan. Heat carefully, stirring to allow the potatoes to steam-dry. Push the hot potatoes through a sieve, mouli or potato ricer.

3.   Place the potatoes to one side of the pan. Set the exposed part of the pan over direct heat and pour in the milk. Add the butter, salt, pepper and nutmeg. Tilt the pan to allow the milk to heat and the butter to melt.

4.   When the milk is steaming beat it into the potatoes. Check the seasoning.

VARIATIONS: Add 2 peeled cloves of garlic to the cooking water in step 1. Mash the garlic in with the potatoes. Substitute olive oil for the butter.

Add 2 tablespoons wholegrain mustard.

Add 2 tablespoons creamed horseradish.

Persian Rice

This recipe requires you to line the base of a saucepan with Bakewell paper. Cut the paper to size and then crumple it up before use – this way you can make sure that the paper lines the saucepan well, as you can press it easily into place.

500g basmati rice

1 tablespoon fine sea salt

olive oil

30g salted butter, melted

1.   Put the rice into a large pan of boiling salted water and cook for 6 minutes or until the rice has just begun to soften.

2.   Drain the rice through a sieve and rinse it well under running cold water – the rice should be cool and the water should run clear.

3.   Line the bottom of a large (but not too deep – you are going to turn the rice out as you would turn out a cake) saucepan with Bakewell paper (see note above).

4.   Drizzle a generous amount of olive oil onto the Bakewell paper and brush over the melted butter. Scatter over the salt.

5.   Scatter the rice into the pan – it should not be packed at all tightly.

6.   Wrap the pan lid in a tea towel – to prevent any steam escaping – cover the pan and cook as slowly as possible for 45 to 60 minutes. The rice should be fluffy when cooked. Leave to stand for 5 minutes before turning the rice out of the pan.

7.   Place a large, flat, round plate over the saucepan. Turn the pan and plate over together. Leave to stand for 10 minutes and then remove the saucepan and very carefully remove the greaseproof paper, it may be necessary to use a blunt knife to scrape the paper – there should be a golden crisp top (tahdig) to the rice cake. If it has not coloured enough tip the rice cake back into the pan and place it over a high heat for 6 minutes. Turn out as before.

This dish has been adapted from a recipe by Sabrina Ghayour.

Savoury Sauces

Bread Sauce

This is a very rich sauce. The quantity of butter may be reduced, and the cream is optional.

½ large onion, peeled

6 cloves

290ml milk

1 bay leaf

10 white peppercorns, or a pinch of freshly ground white pepper

a pinch of freshly grated nutmeg

salt

70g fresh white breadcrumbs

55g butter

2 tablespoons single cream (optional)

1. Stick the cloves into the onion and put with the milk and bay leaf into a saucepan.

2. Add the peppercorns, nutmeg, and a good pinch of salt. Bring to the boil very slowly, then remove from the heat and leave to infuse for 30 minutes. Strain.

3. Re-heat the milk and add the breadcrumbs, butter and the cream, if using. Mix and return to the saucepan.

4. Re-heat the sauce carefully without boiling. If it has become too thick, beat in more hot milk. It should be creamy. Check the seasoning.

Hollandaise Sauce

3 tablespoons wine vinegar

6 black peppercorns

1 bay leaf

1 tablespoon of water

1 blade of mace

2 medium egg yolks

salt

110g unsalted butter

lemon juice

1.   Place the vinegar, peppercorns, bay leaf, water and mace in a small heavy saucepan and reduce by simmering to 1 tablespoon. Strain immediately into a cold bowl.

2.   Cream the egg yolks with a pinch of salt and a nut of the butter and half a teaspoon of the reduction in a small heat-proof bowl. Set in a roasting pan of gently simmering water. Using a wooden spoon, beat the mixture until slightly thickened, taking care that the water immediately around the bowl does not boil. Mix well.

3.   Stir over the heat until slightly thickened. Beat in the butter bit by bit, increasing the temperature as the sauce thickens and you add more butter, but take care that the water does not boil. If the sauce becomes oily in appearance or too thick, add a little more reduction or a few drops of cold water.

4.   When the sauce has become light and thick remove from the heat and beat or whisk for 1 minute. Check the seasoning and add lemon juice, and salt if necessary. Keep warm by standing the bowl in hot water. Serve warm.

Note: Hollandaise sauce will set too firmly if allowed to get cold and it will curdle if overheated. It can be made in larger quantities in either a blender or food processor: simply put the egg yolks and salt into the blender and blend lightly. Add the hot reduction and allow to thicken slightly. Set aside. When ready to serve, pour in warm melted butter, slowly allowing the sauce to thicken as you pour.

Mayonnaise

Mayonnaise is traditionally made by hand using a small bowl and a wooden spoon but it takes quite a long time and I would recommend using a hand-held beater. If making it in a large mixing machine you would need to make at least double this quantity as the whisk rarely reaches to the bottom of the bowl and this can be frustrating.

If the mayonnaise does curdle, start again with a third egg yolk and gradually add the curdled mixture as if adding the oil.

2 medium egg yolks

salt

1 teaspoon dry English mustard

300ml olive oil

squeeze of lemon juice

1 tablespoon white wine vinegar

white pepper

1.   Put the egg yolks, salt and mustard into a small bowl.

2.   Using a hand-held whisk, beat very well and then gradually add the oil.
       To begin with you must add the oil very slowly, making sure that the mixture is beginning to thicken before adding more oil. By the time that half of the oil is added the mixture should be very thick.

3.   Whisk in the lemon juice and then carry on adding the oil rather more quickly, add a little vinegar as you go.

4.   Season to taste, unless you are planning to use the mayonnaise as a base for another sauce and then it will be seasoned at that time.

Note: The dry English mustard is very useful when making mayonnaise as it helps to emulsify the mixture.

French Dressing

There are numerous variations on this recipe. The standard recipe uses 1 part white wine vinegar to 3 parts olive oil. Balsamic vinegar is also delicious.

Place the ingredients in a jam jar with a pinch of dry English mustard and salt and freshly ground black pepper. Screw the lid onto the jar and shake until well emulsified.

The dressing can be kept for a couple of weeks in the refrigerator.

Pesto Dressing

Add a teaspoon of pesto and use a fruit vinegar in place of the wine vinegar.

Dijon Dressing

Add 1 teaspoon of Dijon mustard and use red wine vinegar.

Herb Dressing

Add freshly chopped herbs to the basic recipe.

Garlic Dressing

Add a little crushed garlic to the dressing – do not store.

Pesto

This is very simple to make – if you have a processor the small bowl is the ideal size for making this quantity. It can also be made using a pestle and mortar.

There are a large number of varieties of pesto – the basil can be replaced by rocket, coriander, parsley or dill. Red pesto is made by using chopped sundried tomatoes instead of basil.

Do check the sell-by date on the pine nuts – if stale they give the pesto a bitter flavour.

1 clove garlic, roughly chopped

100g basil leaves, roughly chopped

30g pine nuts, lightly toasted and cooled

30g Parmesan cheese, freshly grated

150ml olive oil

salt

1. Put the garlic and basil into the small bowl of a processor or a mortar and grind to a paste.

2. Add the nuts and cheese and process or grind – the pesto should not get too smooth.

3. Gradually add the oil with the motor running or grinding continually with the pestle. Add salt to taste.

Chilli Sauce

This is the easiest sauce there can possibly be to make – it is also delicious.

150ml chilli dipping sauce (available in most supermarkets)
Finely grated zest and juice of 2 limes

1.	Mix the sauce with the lime zest and juice.

Tartare Sauce

This is particularly delicious served with fried fish such as the goujons of sole (see pages 52–53).

1 quantity mayonnaise (see page 89)

2 tablespoons capers, rinsed and roughly chopped

2 tablespoons gherkins, rinsed and roughly chopped

2 tablespoons parsley, freshly chopped

1 shallot, very finely chopped

squeeze of lemon juice

salt and freshly ground black pepper

1.	Mix all the ingredients together and season to taste.

Mint Sauce

¼–½ bunch of mint

2 tablespoons caster sugar

2 tablespoons hot water

2 tablespoons white wine vinegar

The classic accompaniment to roast lamb.

1. Wash the mint and dry it. Pick the leaves off the stalks and discard the stalks. Finely chop or chiffonade the mint leaves and place in a bowl with the sugar.

2. Add the hot water and leave to stand for 5 minutes to allow the sugar to dissolve. Add the wine vinegar and leave to infuse for a couple of hours. Taste and adjust the sauce with more sugar or vinegar before serving.

Salsa Verde

1 clove garlic, crushed

2 anchovy fillets, roughly chopped

1 shallot, finely chopped

finely grated zest and juice of ½ lemon

1 tablespoon good quality capers, rinsed and roughly chopped

3 tablespoons parsley, freshly chopped

1 tablespoon basil, freshly chopped

150ml olive oil

salt and freshly ground black pepper

maple syrup (optional)

1. Put the garlic and anchovies into the small bowl of a food processor or into a liquidiser. Add the shallot and lemon zest and blitz well.

2. Add the capers, herbs and lemon juice and blitz once more. Add the oil with the motor still running.

3. Season with salt and pepper.

4. Taste and add a drop of maple syrup if the salsa tastes too bitter.

Tomato Sauce

1 tablespoon sunflower oil

1 red onion, finely chopped

2 cloves garlic, chopped

2 x 400g tins chopped tomatoes

150ml red wine

salt and freshly ground black pepper

1. Heat the oil in a saucepan, add the onion and cook very slowly for 5 minutes. Add the garlic and cook for a further minute.

2. Add the tomatoes and rinse out the cans using the red wine. Add the wine to the tomatoes, season well with salt and pepper. Bring the sauce up to the boil and then simmer, uncovered, for 15 minutes.

3. Carefully liquidise the tomato sauce until smooth. It will be necessary to do this in two batches. If the sauce is very hot cover the liquidiser but remove the small central lid. Cover with a tea towel that has been folded over several times – hold the tea towel in place and whizz gently and gradually increase the speed.

Onion Sauce

30g butter

2 large onions, finely chopped

25g flour

1 bay leaf

300ml milk

4 tablespoons double cream

salt and white pepper

1. Melt the butter in a medium sized saucepan, add the onions and sweat very slowly for about 30 minutes until the onions are soft but not brown. Cover the onions with a damp sheet of greaseproof paper and a lid whilst they are sweating – this will help to prevent them from burning but do watch them well and stir them every so often.

2. Remove the pan from the heat – add the flour, mix well and return the pan to the heat and cook for one minute, stirring well to prevent it from catching on the bottom.

3. Remove the pan from the heat and very gradually add the milk, stirring all the time – do not add more milk until the previous addition has been thoroughly incorporated. When you have a smooth mixture add the bay leaf, salt and pepper and return the pan to the heat and bring slowly up to the boil stirring continuously – when the sauce has thickened to coating consistency (the sauce should coat the back of the wooden spoon) simmer it for a minute and then remove the bay leaf and add the cream. Taste and season as necessary.

Puddings

Baked Figs with Mascarpone

8 large ripe figs

150g mascarpone cheese

100g blackberries

4 tablespoons runny honey

70ml good red wine

2 tablespoons demerara sugar

finely grated zest of 1 lemon

1.   Heat the oven to 180C/350F, gas mark 4.

2.   Cut a deep cross into the top of each fig and squeeze them open a bit.

3.   Snugly pack the figs into a baking dish and then stuff spoonfuls of the mascarpone into the open figs. Push one blackberry into the mascarpone and then scatter the other blackberries and some more mascarpone in and around the rest of the figs. Drizzle honey generously over the top and pour enough red wine around the figs to just cover the bottom – the fig juice should combine with the wine and honey to make a sweet and slightly musky sauce.

4.   Just before putting the dish into the oven put a sprinkling of brown sugar over the figs and add the lemon zest.

5.   Put the dish into the oven and bake for about 30 minutes. If it cooks too fast turn it down as you want maximum juice and not to dry out the figs.

This is adapted from a recipe by Shauna Gailey.

Chocolate Fondants

Chocolate fondants are best prepared and chilled at least 1 hour before baking and they can be kept in the refrigerator for up to 24 hours in advance. This recipe makes 5 or 6 fondants (depending on the size of your moulds) so that if you are nervous about the cooking time you can always cook any extra in advance to test the exact time required for your oven.

melted butter

2 tablespoons cocoa powder

120g unsalted butter, cut into dice

120g dark chocolate, broken into pieces

2 eggs and 2 egg yolks (medium sized eggs)

120g caster sugar

3 tablespoons plain flour, sifted

To serve
clotted cream or vanilla ice cream

1. Brush the inside of 6 dariole moulds with the melted butter (brush the butter using upward strokes) and then put the cocoa in one and turn it to coat the inside, holding it over the second mould to catch any that escapes. Do the same with the other moulds. Place in the freezer until ready for use.

2. Put the butter and chocolate into a heat-proof bowl set over, but not touching, a pan of simmering water and stir occasionally until melted. Allow to cool slightly.

3. Using a hand-held electric whisk, mix together the egg, yolk, sugar and a pinch of salt until pale and fluffy. Gently fold in the melted chocolate and butter, and then the flour. Pile into a large measuring jug and pour into the prepared moulds, stopping just short of the top. Leave to chill for 1 hour.

4. Pre-heat the oven to 200C/400F, gas mark 6 and put a baking tray on the middle shelf.

5. Put the fondants onto the prepared baking tray and cook for 12–15 minutes until the tops are set and coming away from the sides of the moulds. Leave to rest for 1–2 minutes and then turn out onto plates.

6. Serve with clotted cream or vanilla ice cream.

Crème Brûlée

Crème brûlées should be prepared a day in advance.

300ml double cream

4 medium egg yolks

1½ tablespoons vanilla sugar (see page 147)

extra caster sugar

1.   Preheat the oven to 150C/300F, gas mark 2.

2.   Put the double cream into a small heavy-based pan.

3.   Place over the heat and bring very gradually almost to the boil, stirring
      occasionally.

4.   Beat the egg yolks with the vanilla sugar. Add the warm cream and mix
      well. Divide the custard between 4 small ramekins (or 3 large ones) and place
      in a roasting tin. Add enough boiling water to come three-quarters of the
      way up the ramekins. Place in the oven for 30 minutes or until the custard
      has just set and a skin has formed.

5.   Refrigerate overnight.

6.   Sprinkle an even layer (about 2mm thick) of caster sugar over each custard.
      Sprinkle lightly with a little water using a spray bottle and then blow torch
      the sugar until lightly and evenly caramelised. Leave to cool but do not
      place in the refrigerator as the caramel will dissolve.

Tarte Tatin

You will need a 24cm heavy-based frying pan that will fit into your oven for this recipe.

The recipe calls for 1.5kgs dessert apples – that is generally about 11 apples. This recipe has been adapted from Leiths *How to Cook*.

Serves 8

For the pastry	For the filling
170g plain flour, sifted	1.5kgs dessert apples
pinch of salt	Finely grated zest of 1 lemon
55g ground rice or semolina	100g unsalted or clarified butter
140g cold unsalted butter, cut into cubes	100g granulated sugar
50g caster sugar	
1 medium egg, beaten	

1. Make the pastry – place the sifted flour in a large bowl, add the salt and ground rice.

2. Add the butter and rub it into the flour (see shortcrust pastry, page 148). Stir in the sugar. Add enough egg to bind the dough together.

3. Shape into a disc, place between two sheets of baking parchment and gently roll to a circle a little larger than your frying pan. It should be about 5mm thick. Place in the refrigerator to rest.

4. Peel and core the apples and cut into neat quarters – sprinkle with the lemon zest.

5. Pre-heat the oven to 190C/375F, gas mark 5.

6. Melt the butter in the frying pan over a low heat. Add the sugar and cook gently until the sugar begins to melt and becomes toffee coloured.

7. Arrange a first layer of apples rounded side down very neatly on top of the butter. The next layer of apples should be the other way up so that they fit neatly on top.

8. Allow the apples to cook over a very moderate heat – this stage may take up to 45 minutes – when the apples begin to cook they will release some

of their juice. This juice will mix with the caramel and it will take a little time before all the juices have become a rich brown colour. Agitate and move the pan to make sure the apples don't burn – you can lift the apples with a palette knife to check how brown the sauce is getting. If you waft your hand over the top of the pan you will be able to smell the steam that rises and you will know when you have beautifully caramelised apples.

9.   Remove from the heat and place the pan on a lipped baking sheet.

10.   Take the pastry out of the refrigerator and remove one sheet of baking parchment. Lay the pastry over the apples, remove the second sheet of paper. Press the pastry down firmly on top of the apples. Remove any excess pastry.

11.   Bake for 25–30 minutes until the pastry is golden brown.

12.   Remove from the oven and allow to cool for 5 minutes. Place a lipped plate on top of the frying pan and very carefully turn them over together – the caramel will be very hot so make sure your arms are protected.

13.   Remove the pan and serve warm.

Arranged Fruit Salad with Mango and Passion Fruit Coulis

1 large ripe mango, peeled and cut into chunks

2 ripe passion fruit, cut in half

3 tablespoons orange juice

4 kiwis peeled and sliced

16 strawberries, hulled and cut in half

100g black grapes, cut in half and seeded

4 small sprigs fresh mint

1.   Process (do not liquidise) the mango flesh with the passion fruit pulp and the orange juice until just smooth.

2.   Sieve the puree onto the base of 4 plates so that each one is well flooded.

3.   Arrange the fruit in an attractive pattern on each plate and garnish with a sprig of mint.

Lemon Posset

600ml double cream

100g caster sugar

finely grated zest and juice of 3 unwaxed lemons

1.   Put the double cream, sugar and lemon zest into a heavy-based pan.

2.   Place over the heat and bring very gradually almost to the boil, stirring occasionally. Reduce the heat and simmer for 2 minutes.

3.   Remove from the heat and add the lemon juice.

4.   Pour into serving glasses and chill for at least 2 hours.

Serves 6

Eton Mess

500g strawberries

1 tablespoon port

4 large meringues, crushed

300ml double cream, lightly whipped

To decorate

a few sprigs of fresh mint

1. Crush the strawberries with a potato masher or fork, reserving 8 strawberries to garnish. Add the port.

2. Mix the prepared strawberries with the crushed meringues and fold in the cream.

3. Pile into individual glasses and decorate with the reserved strawberries and mint.

Rhubarb Tart

For the pastry

butter for greasing

170g plain flour, sifted

40g icing sugar, sifted

140g unsalted butter, melted and slightly cooled

½ teaspoon vanilla extract

finely grated zest of 2 lemons

pinch of salt

For the almond base

50g blanched almonds

2 tablespoons granulated sugar

2 tablespoons plain flour

For the rhubarb filling

300g stems of rhubarb

25g granulated sugar

For the glaze

2 tablespoons apricot jam

1 tablespoon water

1.　Pre-heat the oven to 190C/375F, gas mark 5. Butter a 20cm flan ring.

2.　Make the pastry by mixing all the ingredients until they are thoroughly combined to a soft dough.

3.　Allow to cool in the refrigerator for half an hour or so.

4.　Set the ball of dough in the pan, and press and shape to fit, raising it around the sides of the pan. (This pastry is too soft to roll out with a rolling pin.) Use fingertips to ensure a thin crust, especially around the edges.

5.　Bake blind for 20 minutes (see page 163) then set aside to cool.

6.　In a blender, grind the almonds, adding the sugar and flour to the blender after a few seconds.

7.　Pour the resulting dry mixture evenly over the tart base in the pan.

8.　Slice the rhubarb into very short lengths – about 1.25cm – and arrange in close concentric circles on the almond base. The amount of rhubarb needed to cover the base will depend on how slim the stems are.

9.　Sprinkle the sugar evenly over the rhubarb.

10. Bake for about 25 minutes. The rhubarb should be cooked but not dry or too dark (a slightly toasted colour looks nice, however, and means that the flavour of the rhubarb is fully released).

11. Heat the apricot jam with the water and when well mixed push through a sieve. Keep warm.

12. Remove the tart from the oven and while the tart is still very hot use a spoon or a pastry brush to glaze the rhubarb lightly with the still warm apricot glaze.

This is adapted from a recipe by Tancred Taylor.

Gin and Tonic Jelly with Raspberries

If you decide to use the optional raspberries (see note) this recipe must be begun a day in advance.

Serves 6

300ml water

300g granulated sugar

juice and pared zest of 2 unwaxed lemons

200ml tonic water (not slimline)

200ml gin

about 10 sheets leaf gelatine (see recipe)

1 punnet raspberries (optional)

1. Put the water into a saucepan with the sugar. Place over a gentle heat and allow the sugar to dissolve, add the pared lemon zest. Bring up to the boil and boil for 5 minutes.

2. Remove from the heat and add the lemon juice. Strain through muslin into a measuring jug.

3. Add the tonic water and gin to the sugar syrup.

4. Check how much liquid is in the jug to establish exactly how much gelatine you will need. You should use 1 leaf of gelatine for every 100ml of liquid.

5. Soak the gelatine in a bowl of cold water – the gelatine should be completely covered – and leave to stand for 5 minutes.

6. Heat 50ml of water in a saucepan. Squeeze the gelatine thoroughly, add to the water and remove from the heat. When dissolved, add to the gin and tonic mixture.

7. Set in a mould, or even better it can be poured into martini glasses for serving with 3 raspberries spaced vertically in the glass (see note).

8. Leave to set in the refrigerator.

Note: Setting the raspberries into the jelly can be difficult. Pour a little jelly into the glass – allow it to set and place a raspberry onto the jelly. Half cover the raspberry with more jelly and leave to set again. Add more jelly and leave to set again. Repeat the process two more times.

Strawberry Meringue Roulade

Meringue mixtures are best made using a very good robust electric machine.

The roulade can be made a day in advance but should not be kept in the fridge. Cover it lightly with cling film and put in a cool place. It should only be filled an hour or so before serving.

4 medium egg whites	**For the filling**
220g caster sugar	227ml double cream
20g flaked almonds (optional)	170g Greek yoghurt
	225g/8oz strawberries, hulled
	sprigs of mint

1. Preheat the oven to 200C/400F, gas mark 6.

2. Line a large Swiss roll tin with magic non-stick liner paper (40cm x 28cm/16"x 11") is ideal. However, it is also wise to check that the roulade will fit on your plate – the long side of the tin should be about the length of your plate.

3. Whisk the egg whites in a clean, large bowl with an electric mixer on full speed until very stiff.

4. Gradually add the sugar, one teaspoon at a time and, keeping the mixer on a high speed, whisk well between each addition.

5. Whisk until very stiff and glossy and all the sugar has been added.

6. Spread the meringue mixture evenly into the lined tin and sprinkle with the almonds (if using). Place the tin in the oven and bake for about eight minutes until golden.

7. Reduce the temperature to 160C/320F, gas mark 3, place the roulade on a lower shelf and bake for a further 15 minutes until crisp and firm to the touch.

8. Remove the meringue from the oven, cool for 2 minutes and then turn almond-side down onto a sheet of non-stick baking paper.

9. Remove the paper from the base of the cooked meringue and allow to cool for 20 minutes. Trim the short ends with a serrated-edge knife.

10. Lightly whip the cream and mix with the yoghurt. Spread evenly over the meringue.

11. Slice 3 or 4 of the strawberries finely and arrange them evenly over the cream mixture.

12. Roll up the meringue firmly, using the paper to help you, from the long end of the roulade. It is essential to keep the roll as tight as you can. Roll onto your chosen plate.

13. Cut the remaining strawberries in half and arrange them on top of the meringue. Decorate with mint leaves.

Chocolate Profiteroles

Makes 24–30

For the profiteroles

1 quantity choux pastry (see page 149)

For the filling and topping

300ml double cream, whipped and sweetened with 1 heaped tablespoon sifted icing sugar and a drop of vanilla extract

150g plain chocolate, chopped

15g butter

1 tablespoon golden syrup

1. Preheat the oven to 200C/400F, gas mark 6.

2. Put teaspoons of the choux mixture on a lightly greased baking sheet, about 4cm/1½" apart. Pat down any spikes with a dampened finger.

3. Bake for 20–30 minutes. The profiteroles will puff up and become fairly brown and firm when squeezed. If they are taken out when only slightly brown, they will be soggy when cool.

4. Using a skewer, make a hole the size of a pea in the base of each profiterole and return to the oven placed upside down on the baking sheet for 5 minutes to allow the insides to dry out. Leave to cool completely on a wire rack.

5. When cold, put the sweetened cream into a piping bag fitted with a small plain nozzle. Pipe the cream into the profiteroles through the holes made by the skewer, until well filled.

6. Put the chocolate, butter and syrup into a heat-proof bowl set over, not in, a saucepan of steaming water and leave until melted.

7. Dip the tops of the profiteroles in the melted chocolate, then allow to cool.

Note: If no piping bag is available for filling the profiteroles, they can be split, allowed to dry out, and filled with cream or crème pâtissière when cold, and the icing can be spooned over the top. However, made this way they are messier to eat with the fingers.

French Pancakes (Crêpes)

Makes about 12

120g plain flour

a pinch of salt

1 medium egg, beaten

1 medium egg yolk

300ml milk and water mixed

1 tablespoon oil

To serve

lemon wedges

caster sugar

1. Sift the flour and salt into a mixing bowl, then make a well in the centre exposing the bottom of the bowl.

2. Put the egg and egg yolk with a little of the milk and water into the well.

3. Using a wooden spoon mix the egg and milk and gradually draw in the flour from the sides as you mix.

4. When the mixture reaches the consistency of thick cream add the remaining milk and stir in the oil.

5. The consistency should now be that of thin cream. (Batter can also be made in a blender or food processor, but the mixture can become too bubbly so take care not to overwhizz.)

6. Cover the bowl and refrigerate for 30 minutes. This is done so that the starch cells swell and then when they cook the cells burst and you get a very light pancake.

7. Heat a frying pan or ideally a non-stick crepe pan. Add a little oil and then wipe out the pan – the idea is to use the oil to prevent the pancakes from sticking – pancakes are not fried.

8. Add enough batter to coat the bottom of the pan – swirl the pan to help the batter spread across the bottom of the pan.

9. Place over a medium heat and, when the pancake is lightly brown on the underside, turn it over using a palette knife or your fingers and cook the other side until lightly browned. Pancakes should be very thin – if you can toss a pancake it is probably too thick. The first pancake is rarely perfect.

10.   Make up all the pancakes, turn them out onto a plate and keep them separated with squares of greaseproof paper.

11.   Serve with lemon wedges and plenty of caster sugar.

Note: This recipe uses half milk and half water to make the batter to ensure very light pancakes.

Apple Crumble

1kg Bramley apples

3 tablespoons demerara sugar

1 teaspoon ground cinnamon

finely grated zest and juice of 1 lemon

For the crumble

180g plain flour

pinch of salt

120g butter

60g granulated sugar

1.   Preheat the oven to 200C/400F, gas mark 6.

2.   Make the crumble. Sift the flour with the salt into a large bowl.

3.   Rub in the butter until the mixture resembles coarse breadcrumbs. This can be done initially using two cutlery knives with a scissor action and then by using your fingertips to get even-sized crumbs. Shaking the bowl will help bring the larger lumps to the surface. Add the sugar.

4.   Peel and core the apples. Cut into chunks and pile into a pie dish with the demerara sugar, cinnamon and grated lemon zest and juice.

5.   Sprinkle the crumble mix over the fruit.

6.   Place on a baking sheet and bake for 40 minutes until hot and lightly browned.

Cold Lemon Soufflé

3 medium eggs, separated

140g caster sugar

grated zest and juice of 2 large lemons

3 leaves supermarket gelatine

150ml double cream, lightly whipped

To finish

icing sugar

1. Put the egg yolks into a heat-proof bowl with the sugar and 1½ tablespoons of lemon juice.

2. Put the whites into the bowl of an electric mixer.

3. Soak the leaves of gelatine in a bowl of cold water for 5 minutes – make sure the gelatine is completely covered.

4. Place the bowl with the egg yolks over a saucepan of simmering water – make sure that the base of the bowl does not touch the water. Use a balloon or hand-held electric whisk until the mixture becomes pale and mousse-like. The mixture will have increased in volume a little. Remove from the heat and whisk until cool, and then whisk in the remaining juice and the grated lemon zest.

5. Put enough water into a small saucepan to just cover the base. Squeeze the gelatine to remove excess water. Bring the pan of water up to the boil, add the squeezed gelatine and remove from the heat. Allow the gelatine to melt completely.

6. Stir the dissolved gelatine into the egg yolk mixture. Place the bowl over an ice bath, stir gently with a spatula until nearly at setting point – the mixture will have begun to thicken and when you draw a spatula through the mixture it separates for a couple of seconds before flowing back together.

7. Fold in the lightly whipped cream.

8. Meanwhile whisk the egg whites until fairly stiff – if you lift the whisk the whites should hold their shape but just droop very slightly at the tip.

9. Stir a spoonful of the egg whites into the egg yolk mixture (this will loosen the mixture). Fold in the remaining whites with a large metal spoon.

10.   Pile into a soufflé dish, cover and leave to set for 2–3 hours in the refrigerator.

11.   Just before serving dust with sifted icing sugar.

Tarte au Citron

Serves 6

170g flour quantity pâte sucrée (see page 150)

4 medium eggs

1 medium egg yolk

170g caster sugar

170ml double cream

grated zest and juice of 2 lemons

icing sugar, sifted, for dusting

1.   Preheat the oven to 120C/250F, gas mark ½.

2.   Line a 20cm/8″ flan ring with the pâte sucrée. Refrigerate until firm, then bake blind (see page 163). Remove the lining paper and beans. Turn the oven temperature up to 150C/300F, gas mark 2.

3.   Make the filling: mix the eggs and egg yolk with the sugar until smooth. Pass through a sieve. Stir in the cream. Add the lemon zest and juice. Beat well. The mixture will thicken considerably.

4.   Pour the lemon filling in the pastry case. Bake in the oven for 40–50 minutes until almost set.

5.   When the tart is cooked, remove the flan ring and leave to cool. To serve, dust thickly and evenly with sifted icing sugar.

Salted Caramel Ice Cream

This recipe makes for a soft scoop ice cream.

If using an ice cream maker pour a little vodka into the base (beneath the pot) as it will help to freeze the ice cream.

170g caster sugar

225ml double cream

150ml semi-skimmed milk

4 medium egg yolks

½ teaspoon fine Maldon sea salt

1.   Place a pan on the stove to heat. Once hot, put 140g of the caster sugar into the pan.

2.   Heat, shaking the pan occasionally until the sugar melts to a good caramel colour.

3.   Heat the cream until simmering.

4.   Add the hot double cream slowly and carefully – it will sizzle rather alarmingly. It may go a little lumpy at this stage – don't worry – when most of the lumps have dissolved add the milk.

5.   Meanwhile, in a separate bowl whisk the egg yolks and remaining caster sugar until pale and mousse-like.

6.   Pour the hot caramel on to the sabayon and whisk well, then sieve and chill it.

7.   Add the salt to the chilled mixture and churn in an ice cream machine.

This recipe has been adapted from a recipe by Xanthe Clay.

Mango and Lychee Salad

This is a simple and unusual fruit salad. Mangoes can be hard to peel and slice – a mango cutter is very useful.

2 large ripe mangoes, peeled and neatly sliced

1 x 400g can lychees

finely grated zest of 2 limes

2 red chillis, seeded and finely chopped

1.   Arrange the mangoes very neatly on a large platter – leave a space in the middle.

2.   Drain the lychees of nearly all the juice and pile them into the centre of the mangoes.

3.   Sprinkle the grated lime zest and chillis over the salad.

Sweet Sauces and Icings

Crème Anglaise (English Egg Custard)

300ml milk

1 vanilla pod or a few drops of vanilla extract (unless using vanilla sugar – see note)

3 large egg yolks

1–2 tablespoons caster sugar (vanilla if possible – see note)

1.   Heat the milk and vanilla pod, if using, and bring slowly to the boil. Leave to infuse for 10 minutes. Remove the vanilla pod.

2.   Beat the yolks in a bowl with the sugar. Pour the milk on to the egg yolks, stirring steadily. Mix well and return to the pan.

3.   Stir over a very low heat until the mixture thickens sufficiently to coat the back of a spoon (about 5 minutes). The custard must not boil.

4.   Strain into a bowl, place a piece of greaseproof paper directly on the surface to prevent a skin from forming. Allow to cool.

5.   Add the vanilla extract if using.

Note: Place a vanilla pod in a jar of caster sugar, cover with the lid. As you use the sugar replace it with more sugar.

Crème au Beurre Mousseline

A sugar thermometer is required to make this recipe.

This quantity makes easily enough filling for 50 macaroons or icing to fill and cover a 20cm sponge cake.

115g granulated sugar

135g unsalted butter, softened

4 medium egg yolks

1.   Put the sugar into a small heavy pan with enough water to cover. Place over a gentle heat and allow the sugar to dissolve – do not stir but you can agitate it with the handle of a wooden spoon.

2.   Beat the butter until very soft.

3.   Put the egg yolks into a heat-proof mixing bowl.

4.   When the sugar has completely dissolved increase the heat and bring the sugar syrup up to 108C.

5.   Remove from the heat immediately and, using a hand-held whisk, whisk the sugar syrup onto the egg yolks – be careful not to allow the syrup to touch the whisk.

6.   Whisk until thick – this may take several minutes. The mixture should now be at room temperature. Add it to the butter bit by bit, whisking slowly between each addition. Add flavouring as required. See below.

Note: To flavour add the finely grated zest of lemon, lime or orange. Alternatively add 1 or 2 teaspoons of very strong warm expresso to the butter just before you add it to the egg yolk mousse.

Caramel Sauce

Sugar syrups are made with granulated sugar as the crystals are larger than in caster sugar and thus the water can flow more freely between the crystals. This means that it dissolves more quickly and the sugar is less likely to 'clump' at the bottom of the pan. If you are making caramel without water (see salted caramel ice cream) then use caster, rather than granulated, sugar as the smaller crystals dissolve more quickly.

250g granulated sugar

250ml water

1.   Put the sugar into a heavy saucepan with half of the water.

2.   Place over a very gentle heat. Dissolve the sugar without letting the water come to the boil. Use the handle of a wooden spoon to agitate the sugar and to prevent it from forming a clump at the bottom of the pan but do not stir it. Avoid letting the syrup splash up the sides. Once dissolved use a pastry brush dipped in cold water to brush down the sides of the pan to return any sugar crystals to the pan.

3.   Bring the syrup gently up to the boil until it is a good caramel colour.

4.   Cover your hand with a dry tea towel and tip in the remaining water – take care as it will fizz dangerously.

5.   Place over a gentle heat – gently swirling the pan if necessary – until all the lumps have disappeared. Allow to cool.

Cakes, Buns, Biscuits and Breads

Chocolate Chip Cookies

Makes 16

110g unsalted butter, softened

65g granulated sugar

65g soft light brown sugar

1 large egg, lightly beaten

1 teaspoon vanilla extract

175g plain flour, sifted

½ teaspoon baking powder

100g dark chocolate chips

1. Preheat the oven to 190C/375F, gas mark 5. Line 2 baking sheets with 'Bake-O-Glide' paper. (If not available use silicone paper.)

2. Put the butter into a mixing bowl and, using a hand-held whisk, whisk until very creamy – add the sugars and whisk until fluffy.

3. Gradually beat in the beaten egg. Add the vanilla extract. Add the sifted flour and baking powder – stir until smooth and then fold in the chocolate chips. Shape, using your hands, into 16 balls.

4. If the dough is very sticky put it into the freezer for 15 minutes or so.

5. Place on the baking sheets and flatten into circles – the dough will spread so make sure that they are well spaced.

6. Bake for 10 to 12 minutes until just beginning to brown at the edges. If you are cooking them on different shelves it is a good idea to swap the baking sheets around halfway through cooking.

7. Remove from the oven – leave to cool and harden for 2 minutes on the baking sheet and then place on a wire rack to cool completely.

8. The cookies should be firm at the edges but chewy in the centre.

Carrot Cake

Makes a 20cm/8" cake

250ml vegetable oil, plus extra for greasing

4 medium eggs, beaten

225g soft light brown sugar

140g carrots, peeled and finely grated

225g self-raising flour

½ teaspoon bicarbonate of soda

1½ teaspoon ground cinnamon

½ teaspoon ground ginger

For the icing

80g unsalted butter, softened

85g icing sugar, sifted

180g good quality full-fat cream cheese

1 teaspoon vanilla extract

To decorate

8 walnut halves (optional)

1. Preheat the oven to 180C/350F, gas mark 4. Lightly oil 2 x 200cm/8" sandwich tins and line the bases with discs of baking parchment.

2. In a large bowl, stir together the oil, eggs and sugar.

3. Stir in the carrots.

4. Sift the flour, bicarbonate of soda, cinnamon and ginger onto a large piece of greaseproof paper and tip into the egg and sugar mixture. Whisk together until all the flour is incorporated.

5. Turn the mixture into the prepared tins.

6. Bake in the centre of the oven for 25–30 minutes or until the cakes spring back when pressed lightly in the centre and a wooden cocktail stick inserted into the centre comes out clean. Leave to stand for 5 minutes.

7. Release the cakes from the tins and turn out onto a wire rack. Leave to cool, then remove the lining paper.

8. Make the icing: beat the butter until very soft, add the icing sugar and beat together until smooth. Add the cream cheese and beat until just mixed – if over-beaten at this stage the icing may go runny.

9. Stir in the vanilla extract. Use the icing to fill the cake and ice the top. Garnish with the walnut halves, if desired.

Banana Cake

This cake is good for using over-ripe bananas.

oil for greasing

4 ripe bananas

150g light brown sugar

3 medium eggs, beaten

150ml sunflower oil

75ml milk

225g self-raising flour, sifted

100g dried fruit and nuts, e.g. pecan nuts and dried dates, chopped (optional)

To finish

10 pecan halves

1. Preheat the oven to 170C/325F, gas mark 3 and oil a non-stick 1kg loaf tin.

2. Peel, and mash the bananas in a large bowl (it is fine for there to be some lumps).

3. Beat in the sugar, eggs, oil and milk. Whisk in the self-raising flour until smooth.

4. Stir in the dried fruit and nuts – if using.

5. Pour the mixture into the loaf tin. Arrange the pecan halves on the top and bake in the oven for 1½ hours until light brown on top and when you insert a skewer it comes out clean.

6. Leave to cool in the tin for 5 minutes and then turn out onto a wire rack.

Chocolate Brownies

Makes 16

140g unsalted butter, cut into small pieces

200g dark chocolate, chopped

225g caster sugar

1 teaspoon vanilla extract

pinch of salt

2 large eggs at room temperature

1 large egg yolk at room temperature

85g plain flour, sifted

1. Preheat the oven to 180C/350F, gas mark 4. Line a 20cm square tin with silicone paper.

2. In a bowl set over, not in, a pan of simmering water, melt the butter and the chocolate together. Remove the pan from the heat and allow to cool slightly. Whisk in the sugar and then the vanilla extract and salt. The mixture will be somewhat grainy.

3. Whisk in the beaten eggs and egg yolk, until well mixed. Add the sifted flour, stir well until thick and smooth. Pour into the prepared tin and bake for 30–35 minutes or until a knife inserted in the middle comes out with moist crumbs (not wet batter) clinging to it.

4. Allow the brownies to cool before cutting into squares with a sharp knife.

Rich Chocolate Cake

This cake can be stored for 4 days wrapped in tin foil or frozen for up to 2 months.

Makes a 30cm cake

butter for greasing

650g unsalted butter, cut into small pieces

650g dark chocolate, chopped

100ml espresso

3 teaspoons vanilla extract

950g soft brown sugar

650g plain flour, sifted

pinch of salt

2 teaspoons baking powder, sifted

2 teaspoons bicarbonate of soda, sifted

10 medium eggs at room temperature, beaten

2 x 284ml soured cream

1. Preheat the oven to 180C/350F, gas mark 4. Butter and double line a 30cm round tin with silicone paper.

2. In a bowl set over, not in, a pan of simmering water, melt the butter and the chocolate together. Add the coffee and vanilla. Remove the pan from the heat and allow to cool slightly.

3. Mix together the sugar, flour, salt and baking powder in a large bowl. If there are lumps in the sugar break them up with your fingertips.

4. Mix the eggs and soured cream together and stir into the flour mix. Add the chocolate mix and stir until you have a smooth batter.

5. Pile into the cake tin and bake for 2½ hours. Leave to cool in the cake tin.

6. Ice as required.

Macaroons

The key to good macaroons is to be very accurate with all your measurements and timing. If you want coloured macaroons it is necessary to add food colouring. Do buy natural food colourings – available in good supermarkets. This recipe calls for vanilla sugar – this is made by placing a vanilla pod in a jar of caster sugar. Every time you use some of the sugar you can top it up with more sugar.

This recipe requires the use of a sugar thermometer.

200g ground almonds

200g icing sugar

160g egg whites

75ml water

200g vanilla sugar

For the filling

good quality jam

or crème au beurre mousseline (see page 122)

1. Line 2 large baking sheets with 'Bake-O-Glide' paper.

2. Place the icing sugar and ground almonds in a food processor and pulse until very fine. Pass through a sieve. (This is not absolutely necessary but it does help to improve the final appearance of the macaroons, giving them a smoother finish.)

3. Put the mixture into a mixing bowl and beat in exactly half of the egg whites until you have a smooth paste.

4. Meanwhile place the water and vanilla sugar in a small saucepan and place over a gentle heat. The water must not boil until all the sugar has dissolved – a heat diffuser is very useful when making sugar syrups. When the sugar has completely dissolved bring the syrup up to the boil and remove from the heat when it reaches 115C.

5. When the sugar syrup is reaching the correct temperature (i.e. when it is about 110C) start to whisk the egg whites with a hand-held electric whisk – they should get to medium/stiff peak consistency (see note) just as the syrup reaches 115C.

6. Pour the sugar syrup onto the egg whites being careful not to let the syrup touch the whisk. Whisk until doubled in volume, shiny and quite stiff.

7. Stir one third of the mixture vigorously into the almond paste. Carefully fold

in the remaining meringue. It should be a smooth mixture by now.

8.   Preheat the oven to 160C/325F, gas mark 3. (See note 2.)

9.   Fill a piping bag fitted with a plain nozzle with the macaroon mixture and pipe small discs onto the prepared trays – you should expect to make about 90–100 macaroons. Leave them to stand for 20–30 minutes – they should feel as though they have developed a skin. Give the baking sheet a tap on the work surface – to remove any little pockets of air.

10. Bake for 15–20 minutes until crisp. If you are cooking them on two shelves swap the trays around after about 10 minutes.

11. Slide the macaroons off the baking tray onto a cool work surface and leave them to cool completely.

12. Sandwich them together using good quality jam or crème au beurre mousseline. (See page 122.)

Note 1: Soft peak is when the whisk is lifted the peak falls over itself, medium peak is when the peak begins to fall but then steadies itself, stiff peak is when the peak stays firm. For macaroons the peak should be almost stiff but with a very faint fall before steadying itself.

Note 2: Macaroons will crack if cooked at too high a temperature – a fan-assisted electric oven tends to be slightly more reliable than a gas one for baking macaroons.

Focaccia

500g strong white bread flour

5g fine salt

7g powdered dried fast action yeast

250ml warm water

130ml olive oil

To finish

rosemary sprigs, soaked in olive oil

a generous drizzle of olive oil

coarse sea salt

1. Sift the flour with the salt into a large bowl. Make a well in the centre and add the yeast, water and olive oil. Quickly mix the ingredients together to form a soft dough. Turn onto a floured surface and knead for 5 minutes.

2. Roll it into a rough oval about 2cm thick, lightly oil a shallow baking tray and slip the rolled dough onto to the baking sheet. Leave to prove, covered with greased cling film, in a warm place, for about an hour.

3. Meanwhile preheat the oven to its highest setting.

4. When the dough looks soft and pillowy make about 12 indentations in the dough with your finger. Place a sprig of rosemary in each dent. Bake for 10 minutes. Turn the oven down to 200C/400F, gas mark 6.

5. Bake for 10–15 minutes. Remove from the oven and place on a wire rack. Drizzle generously with olive oil and coarse sea salt. Cover with a clean tea towel.

Note: This mixture can be made in a heavy electric mixer using a dough hook. Knead for 2 minutes in the machine and then lightly knead on a floured surface until smooth.

Croissants

This has been adapted from a Richard Bertinet and a Leiths School recipe.

You will need to make a template for use when cutting the dough – it should be an elongated triangle that is 12cm by 15cm measured vertically from the middle of the base – I am sure Lakeland will be selling them soon.

These croissants have to be prepared the day they are baked.

500g strong flour

1½ teaspoons salt

50g caster sugar

10g fast action dried yeast

125ml water

125ml full fat milk, cold

1 small egg, beaten

250g unsalted butter, cold

For the glaze

1 egg yolk

1 tablespoon milk

1.   Sift the flour into a large mixing bowl or into the bowl of a KitchenAid. Add the salt, sugar and yeast. Mix together the water, milk and egg and add to the flour.

2.   If you are making the dough by hand, mix to a soft, slightly sticky dough – turn onto a floured board and knead for 6 minutes until smooth and springy. If using a dough hook mix the ingredients together using the dough hook – they will come together very quickly and knead in the bowl for 3 minutes – remove from the bowl and knead for a further minute or two on a lightly floured work surface.

3.   Place the dough on a very lightly oiled plate and then cover loosely but thoroughly with very lightly oiled cling film. Refrigerate overnight.

4.   Place the butter between 2 pieces of silicone paper and using a rolling pin bat it into a 12cm square – the size doesn't have to be too accurate at this point but it should be of a uniform thickness. Refrigerate overnight.

5.   The next day remove the butter dough from the refrigerator and quickly

and carefully shape the dough into a ball with no folds or creases on the bottom of the ball. The dough must not be at all overworked at this stage.

6.   Cut a cross in the top halfway through the dough. Pull each corner of the cut dough away from the dough ball and roll the first corner into flap a quarter of the thickness off the dough ball. (The flap should be of such a size that when folded over the centre of the dough ball it will exactly cover the square centre – do not fold it over the dough yet.) Repeat with the other three flaps.

7.   When the butter is still cold but pliable (bend it a little – it should not crack) resize it so that is exactly the same size as the centre of the dough. Remove from the silicone paper and place the butter in the centre of the dough.

8.   Fold each flap in turn over the butter – each flap should cover the butter completely and evenly.

9.   Flour the work surface and 'ridge' the dough (do not roll it, simply press down firmly and evenly) until you have a rectangle. Using short sharp strokes roll until the dough is three times as long as it is wide.

10.   Be careful to keep the sides neat – perfectionism will pay dividends when making croissants. Brush off any excess flour and fold the dough into three – bring the bottom third up over the middle third and bring down the top third – make sure that the corners are aligned.

11.   Give the dough a quarter turn so that the folded edge of the dough is on your right. Wrap loosely in cling film and refrigerate for 15 minutes.

12.   Repeat steps 10 and 11 twice. If the dough is rested for more than 15 minutes let it stand for a while before rolling and folding it. This is because if the butter gets too hard when you roll the dough it may break through the dough – you never want to see any streaks of butter as you roll and fold the dough.

13.   After the third roll and fold, roll the dough into a large rectangle that is about 4mm thick – at this point the dough can be chilled again – even overnight if preferred.

14.   Cut the dough into triangles using your template. Make a 1.25cm deep cut at the centre of the base of the triangle.

15.   Place the triangle on the work surface with the longer point away from you and then, stretching the two shorter points away from each other, roll up the triangle into a croissant shape – you should end up with the point underneath the croissant. Bring the two 'wings' of the croissant as close to each other as possible – they will separate out as they cook – and place on a baking sheet.

16.   Roll up the remaining croissants. Cover lightly with cling film and leave to prove at room temperature for 1 hour. The room temperature should be about 19C – if it is too hot the butter could melt and the croissants will be greasy.

17.   Pre-heat the oven to 200C/400F, gas mark 6.

18.   Mix together the egg yolk and milk.

19.   The croissants are ready to make when they have risen a little, they will almost wobble if the baking sheet is agitated and if you prod them with a finger the indentation will remain.

20.   Glaze the croissants very carefully using a pastry brush – do not glaze where the dough has been folded to form the rolls – it will create uneven rising.

21.   Bake for 10 minutes, reduce the temperature to 190C/375F, gas mark 5 and bake for a further 15–20 minutes – watch them carefully and if they are browning too much cover with a piece of greaseproof paper.

22.   Remove from the oven and leave to cool on a wire rack.

Scones

The amount of milk needed can vary a little – you might need a little more or less than called for in the recipe. Use just enough to make a soft, spongy dough.

Makes 8–10 large scones

450g self-raising flour

large pinch salt

110g cold salted butter, cut into cubes

60g caster sugar

240–250ml milk

1 egg, beaten, to glaze

To serve

clotted cream

strawberry jam

1.   Preheat the oven to 220C/425F, gas mark 7. Flour a baking sheet.

2.   Sift the flour with the salt into a large bowl.

3.   Rub in the butter until the mixture resembles breadcrumbs. Stir in the sugar.

4.   Make a deep well in the flour, pour in the milk and mix to a soft, spongy dough with a knife.

5.   On a floured surface, knead the dough lightly until it is smooth. Roll out until about 2.5cm/1″ thick and stamp into rounds with a pastry cutter. Place on a floured baking sheet.

6.   Brush the top of the scones with beaten egg.

7.   Bake at the top of the oven for 20 minutes, or until well risen and brown. Leave to cool on a wire rack.

8.   Serve with clotted cream and strawberry jam.

Fruit Scones

Add 30g sultanas or other dried fruit once the butter has been rubbed in.

Cheese Scones

Reduce the butter by half, omit the sugar and add 45g of grated mature Cheddar just before you add the milk.

Drop Scones

These are traditionally served with butter and jam but you can also use the same recipe and then serve them as a canapé topped with soured cream, smoked salmon and fresh dill.

Makes about 30

200g plain flour

a pinch of salt

4 teaspoons baking powder

2 medium eggs, separated

300ml milk

2 tablespoons melted butter, cooled

To serve

butter

jam

1.	Sift the flour, salt and baking powder into a mixing bowl, make a well in the centre exposing the bottom of the bowl.

2.	Put the egg yolks with a little of the milk into the well.

3.	Using a wooden spoon mix the egg and milk and gradually draw in the flour from the sides as you mix. Gradually add the remaining milk, stirring well as you pour until the mixture is smooth and is the consistency of thick cream. Stir in the melted butter.

4.	Whisk the egg whites until just stiff – soft/medium peak – and fold into the batter.

5.	Heat a frying pan. Add a little oil and then wipe out the pan – the idea is to use the oil to prevent the drop scones from sticking.

6.	When really hot, drop spoonfuls of the batter onto the surface, keeping them well separated.

7.	Cook for 2 to 3 minutes – bubbles should rise to the surface of the drop scones – turn over using a fish slice and allow to brown on the other side.

8.	Keep warm covered with a tea towel.

Shortbread

Makes 8 petticoat tails

100g unsalted butter, softened

50g caster sugar

130g plain flour, sifted

30g ground rice, sifted

To finish

extra caster sugar

1. Preheat the oven to 170C/325F, gas mark 3.

2. Put the butter into a mixing bowl and beat until very creamy – add the sugar and beat until fluffy.

3. Add the sifted flour and ground rice – stir until smooth, you may need to use the back of the spoon to mash it into a smooth mixture.

4. Place on a baking sheet and carefully shape into a 18cm/7" circle – you can flatten the mixture carefully with a wooden spoon but try to keep it as a circle.

5. Crimp the edges and mark into 8 wedges.

6. Put it into the refrigerator for 15 minutes or so.

7. Sprinkle evenly with caster sugar and bake for 20–25 minutes until a pale biscuit colour.

8. Remove from the oven – using a palette knife loosen the biscuit from the base but leave to cool and harden for 5 minutes on the baking sheet and then place on a wire rack to cool completely.

This has been adapted from Leiths *How to Cook*

Sourdough Bread

This recipe has been adapted from many recipes and advice from many friends, particularly James Backhouse and Roland Carreras.

To check that your starter is ready do the 'float' test: simply place a small teaspoonful of starter in a cup of water and it should float for at least 20 seconds. If it doesn't float give the starter a firm stir and try again using a cup of clean water. If it still doesn't float see page 165.

In this recipe I have used weight rather than volume measurements for the liquid ingredients as it is a more accurate method of getting exact quantities.

The process for making this bread is unusual and pretty time consuming but well worth the effort. If you enjoy making sourdough I would recommend buying a baking cloche. You will not need to create a steamy atmosphere (see step 8) if using a cloche.

100g starter (see page 165), at room temperature

320ml warm water

500g strong organic white bread flour

10g salt mixed with 20g water – it is important that the salt is free from anti-caking ingredients

rice flour for dusting the baneton

semolina for dusting the cloche

1. Put the starter into a large bowl with the water – whisk lightly with a balloon whisk and then add the flour. Using a dough scraper mix to a rough dough making sure that all the flour is incorporated. Cover with a damp tea towel and leave to stand for 1 hour.
2. Put fingerprints into the dough, pour over the salty water and knead for 4–5 minutes.
3. Leave the dough for one hour and then every half hour or so for the next 3 hours lift the dough from a corner as high as you can and fold it back onto the dough in the mixing bowl. Give the bowl a quarter turn and repeat the stretching and folding action. Turn the bowl twice more so that you have done 4 stretches. (Keep the dough covered when not folding and turning.) After the final stretch and turn the dough should be smooth and elastic.
4. Flour a proving basket very lightly with rice flour. The dough is less likely to stick to the basket if you use rice rather than wheat flour.
5. Knead the dough lightly until just smooth and place it into the basket. If you don't have a proving basket shape the dough into an oval and place on a well-floured tea towel placed on a tray.
6. Leave to rise covered with a damp tea towel for 6 hours in a coolish kitchen. Then leave it the fridge overnight.
7. Preheat the oven to 250C/425F, gas mark 8.
8. Place your baking stone (or a baking sheet) into the oven, and place a roasting

pan filled with boiling water (this is to create a steamy atmosphere) into the bottom of the oven. If you put a few bits of metal such as a fish slice and a basting spoon into the water you get a very steamy atmosphere. (You don't need the steamy water if using a cloche.)

9. When the dough has risen close to the top of the basket and feels spongy remove the tea towel; then you will have to turn the dough upside down from the basket onto the baking stone – dust the stone with semolina (far better than flour as the bread never sticks to the stone) and carefully turn the dough out. This is can be quite hard – the stone is hot and you must loosen the dough very carefully so that none of it sticks to the basket. If it has been in the fridge overnight it turns out very easily. If using a baking sheet, simply place your dough onto the hot baking sheet dusted with semolina.

10. With a very sharp knife (I have found that a razor blade is good for this) score a pattern onto the top of the dough – this is important – you have to cut through the top of the dough not just mark a pattern – the angle of the knife should be about 30 degrees – it has to be done quickly and smoothly – the cutting ensures even rising and a good crust. Cover the bread with something large enough for the dough to rise in, such as an upturned Le Creuset pot. The best thing is to invest in a bread cloche and then you don't have to create the steamy atmosphere.

11. Bake for 25 minutes or until well risen. Carefully remove your cover and bake for a further 20–30 minutes. To test if it is cooked tap the bottom of the dough – it should sound hollow – if it is not cooked reduce the oven temperature and check every 5 minutes until the bread is cooked. It will be a very dark brown.
Leave to cool on a wire rack.

Note 1: The salt is added an hour after the dough has been mixed as salt can inhibit rising and this gives the natural yeast a head start.
Note 2: Rice flour is generally found in the gluten-free section in supermarkets.

Spelt Bread

500g wholegrain spelt flour

½ teaspoon salt

1 teaspoon quick yeast

1 teaspoon caster sugar

300ml water at blood temperature

1 tablespoon olive oil

1. Sift the flour with the salt into a large bowl. Add any grains left in the sieve to the bowl.

2. Add the yeast and sugar.

3. Add the water and when almost mixed together add the oil and knead well on a floured surface for two to three minutes.

4. Place in a clean bowl, cover with a clean cloth and leave to rise until doubled in bulk for one hour in a warm place.

5. Preheat the oven to 220C/425F, gas mark 7. Oil a 1kg loaf tin.

6. Turn the dough out onto a floured surface and knead for two to three minutes.

7. Shape the dough and place it in the prepared loaf tin.

8. Cover and leave to rise for a further 25 minutes.

9. Bake for 30 minutes.

10. Remove from the tin. The bread should sound hollow when tapped on the underside. Leave to cool on a wire rack.

Basic Recipes

Orange Marmalade

It is very important to use preserving sugar not jam sugar – jam sugar contains pectin but oranges are high in pectin so it is not necessary and you get a much clearer marmalade than you would if you had used jam sugar. Also it is easy to overset the marmalade if you use jam sugar.

2kg Seville oranges

4 lemons

4.5 litres water

4kg preserving sugar

You will need a large preserving pot, 20 sterilised jam jars and a pack of jam jar covers.

1. Put the whole fruit into a basin of lukewarm water and wash them well.

2. Put the washed fruit into a very large preserving pan. Add the water and put a lid onto the pan so that the oranges don't float above the water. Bring to the boil and simmer for one and a half to two hours. You should be able to pierce the skin with a skewer when they are ready.

3. Pre-heat the oven to 140C/300F, gas mark 3.

4. Using a slotted spoon remove the fruit to a plate and leave to cool slightly.

5. Cut the fruit into quarters and scrape the pulp and pips into the pan of water with any fruit juice. Bring up to the boil for 10 minutes and strain, using a sieve and a piece of sterilised muslin, keep the juice but discard the pulp.

6. Put the sugar into a heat-proof container and place in the oven until warmed through.

7. Put the jam jars into the oven until warm.

8. Chop the fruit peel as finely or as coarsely as preferred and put into the pan of water. Bring to the boil and add the still warm sugar. Stir gently until the sugar has dissolved. Bring to the boil and simmer for about half an hour or until setting point has been reached. See note below.

9.   Leave the marmalade to stand for a while and when the fruit is suspended throughout the mixture ladle it carefully into the clean still warm jars.

10.   Seal the jars immediately following the instructions on the packet.

11.   If the jars are a little sticky on the outside clean them with a warm cloth before letting them get completely cold.

Note: Setting point. Put 5 or 6 saucers in the freezer before you start making the marmalade.

When you think the marmalade is ready put a small spoonful onto a cold saucer – leave it for 30 seconds and then push it with your finger – if it wrinkles the marmalade is ready. Whilst doing the wrinkle test take the marmalade off the heat to prevent it cooking further. If the setting point hasn't been reached, return to the heat and repeat until the setting point has been reached.

I prefer marmalade to be quite runny and if you too like it runny put a spoonful onto a saucer and just leave it to stand for a minute or two. If it looks as though it is going a little jelly-like it is ready.

This recipe has been adapted from a recipe by Nigella Lawson.

Vanilla Sugar

I always have a pot of vanilla sugar in my kitchen.

Simply fill a large airtight container with caster sugar and add two whole vanilla pods. Leave it for a couple of days before use.

As you use the sugar simply replace it with plain caster sugar which will become vanilla-flavoured in no time at all.

Rich Shortcrust Pastry

170g plain flour

pinch of salt

100g cold butter, cut into 1cm cubes

1 medium egg yolk

very cold water to mix

1. Sift the flour with the salt into a large bowl.

2. Rub in the butter until the mixture resembles coarse breadcrumbs. This can be done initially using two cutlery knives working with a scissor action (this is to keep the pastry as cool as possible) and then by using fingertips to get even-sized crumbs. Shaking the bowl will bring the larger lumps of butter to the surface.

3. Mix the egg yolk with 1½-2 tablespoons of water and add to the flour mixture.

4. Mix to a firm dough, first with a knife, and finally with one hand. It may be necessary to add more water but the pastry should not be too damp. Shape into a ball and then flatten into a disc.

5. Chill, wrapped, in the refrigerator for 30 minutes before using.

Choux Pastry

This recipe is for sweet choux pastry for making puddings such as chocolate profiteroles (see pages 112–113). For savoury dishes omit the sugar. It is very important to weigh the ingredients accurately when making choux pastry.

85g butter, cut into cubes

220ml water

100g flour, very well sifted

pinch of salt

1 tablespoon caster sugar

3 medium eggs, beaten

1.   Put the butter and water into a saucepan and place over a gentle heat. Allow the butter to melt without boiling the water. As soon as the butter has melted bring the water to a rolling boil and tip in the very well sifted flour with the salt.

2.   Immediately remove the pan from the heat and beat the mixture hard with a wooden spoon. Add the sugar and continue to beat until the mixture is smooth and leaves the side of the pan.

3.   Pile the mixture onto a plate and spread it flat. Leave to get cold.

4.   Put the panade (the butter, flour and water mixture) back into the saucepan or into a mixing bowl and gradually add the beaten egg, beating well between each addition. The mixture should become smooth, shiny and of dropping consistency – that is, the mixture will drop reluctantly off the wooden spoon when slightly jerked. It may not be necessary to add all the egg – however, the more egg you can incorporate the better the pastry. This beating can be done using a hand-held whisk.

5.   Use as required.

Pâte Sucrée

This makes more than plenty of pastry to line a 20cm flan.

170g plain flour

a pinch of salt

85g unsalted butter, softened but cool

2 medium egg yolks

85g caster sugar

2 drops of vanilla extract

1. Sift the flour and salt onto the work surface. Make a very large well in the centre, exposing the work surface, and put the butter into it.

2. Using the fingertips of one hand, 'peck' at the butter until it softens but does not get greasy. You don't want any hard lumps of butter left. When soft add the sugar and 'peck' until it is incorporated thoroughly. Add the egg yolks and vanilla and continue to 'peck' until they are completely mixed in – there should be no streakiness in the mixture.

3. Using a palette knife, gradually flick the flour onto the butter mix and then using the side of the palette knife chop the flour into the butter mixture. Sometimes you will need to lift some of the flour from the work surface onto the butter mixture. Continue until there are no dry floury bits – you should have unincorporated pieces of dough by now.

4. Shape the pastry into a rough sausage shape and using a dough scraper or palette knife scrape at a little of the dough at a time so that it becomes incorporated. Set aside the dough as you scrape. It can be removed from the palette knife with a cutlery knife.

5. Bring the pastry together gently to form a ball and then shape into a flat disc. Wrap in cling film and chill for 30 minutes.

Poached Eggs on Toast

Eggs for poaching must be very fresh; if not, a little vinegar can be added to the water to help the white coagulate, but too much vinegar will have an adverse effect on the taste. Ideally clean water should be used for poaching each egg.

Serves 4

4 very fresh cold eggs

4 slices of fresh toast, buttered

1 teaspoon white wine vinegar (optional)

salt and freshly ground black pepper

1. Fill a large saucepan with water and vinegar, if using, and bring to simmering point.

2. Crack an egg into a cup.

3. Raise the temperature so that the water bubbles gently. Using a wooden spoon create a whirlpool by stirring the water vigorously. Holding the cup as near to the water as possible, tip the egg into the centre of the whirlpool.

4. Reduce the temperature and using a slotted spoon carefully draw the egg white close to the yolk.

5. Poach each egg for 2–3 minutes until the white is set, but the yolk is still soft.

6. Lift out with the slotted spoon, drain thoroughly by shaking the slotted spoon and trim the egg whites neatly with a pair of scissors if they are ragged at the edges.

7. Place each egg on a piece of toast and sprinkle with salt and pepper.

Pasta

Pasta is fun to make but I strongly recommend using an electric attachment to roll and cut the dough. If using a machine, roll out all the pasta (hang the pasta to dry – I use an indoor washing line dusted with flour) and then cut it using the cutting attachment. Be careful not to let the rolled out pieces of dough touch each other – they will stick together.

Once cut the pasta can be kept on trays – dust the tray with semolina and turn the cut pasta in the semolina – when you cook the pasta shake off all the excess semolina.

Steps 1 and 2 of the recipe can be made in a food processor – whizz the flour, eggs and oil together until the mixture looks like coarse crumbs. Turn it out onto a floured work surface and then knead as in step 3.

Never wash a pasta machine – just brush it clean.

400g strong '00' flour

4 large eggs

1 tablespoon oil

semolina

1. Sift the flour on to a clean work surface. Make a large well in the centre and put in the eggs and oil.

2. Using the fingers of one hand, mix together the eggs and oil and gradually draw in the flour, to make very stiff dough.

3. Knead until fairly smooth (about 10 minutes). Wrap in cling film and leave to relax in a cool place (not the refrigerator) for 45 minutes.

4. Remove a small piece of dough and roll it out until paper-thin. Cut into the required shape. Keep the remaining dough covered at all times.

5. Allow to dry (unless making ravioli), hanging over a chair back if long noodles, or lying on a wire rack or dry tea towel if small ones, for at least 10 minutes before cooking. Ravioli is dried after stuffing.

Note: If more or less pasta is required the recipe can be altered on a pro-rata basis, for example a 340g quantity of flour calls for 3 eggs and 1 scant tablespoon of oil. If making pasta in advance it can be kept in the refrigerator but should be allowed to get back up to room temperature for about 20 minutes before rolling.

Boiled Eggs

Eggs are often boiled, yet there is considerable confusion about the correct method of doing this. The easiest and most foolproof is as follows:

1. Bring a pan of water to the boil. Have the eggs at room temperature. (If chilled, add 30 seconds to cooking time.)

2. Carefully lower the eggs into the water on a perforated spoon.

3. Time the cooking from the moment of immersion, keeping the water simmering or gently boiling, and not boiling too vigorously, which tends to crack the shells and toughen the whites. Four minutes will cook a medium sized egg until the white is barely set; indeed, the white closest to the yolk will still be slightly jelly-like. Four and a half minutes gives a runny yolk and a just-set white. Five minutes give a well-set white and moist but runny yolk (set on the rim and thick but wet inside). Eight minutes give a hard-boiled egg with a set, but still moist, yolk. Twelve minutes will give a yolk sufficiently cooked to be dry and crumbly when mashed.

Chicken Stock

Stock should be made using raw bones – it can be made from bones leftover from a roast but the flavour will be less intense.

Never add salt to a stock – stock is generally reduced, by boiling rapidly, for storage and it is hard to gauge the correct quantity of salt.

Never use starchy vegetables in a stock as they can make the stock cloudy.

This recipe is for white stock – if you want brown stock the bones and vegetables are browned in a little oil in a hot oven then transferred to the stock-pot.

Button mushrooms are added to a stock as they absorb some of the fat.

Veal bones are used in stock-making as they make the resulting stock more gelatinous as the young bones are full of collagen.

2kgs chicken bones, trimmed of excess fat

1kg veal bones, chopped and trimmed of excess fat

3 onions, peeled and quartered

2 carrots, cut into large chunks

4 celery sticks, cut thickly

few sprigs of thyme

2 bay leaves

parsley stalk, bruised

6 peppercorns

handful of button mushrooms, halved

1. Put the bones into a tall stock-pot and cover with water and bring slowly up to the boil. You will see that the liquid is acquiring a scum so as the water comes up to the boil splash in about 500ml of cold water – this will lower the temperature and solidify the fat and scum which will come to the surface. Using a large metal spoon skim off as much of the scum as you possibly can.

2. Add the remaining ingredients to the stockpot, cover with cold water and bring slowly up to the boil. Simmer for 3 hours skimming it occasionally – if necessary you can splash in a second 500ml of cold water to help you skim off the fat. (This technique is called dépouiller.)

3.   Pour through a fine sieve into a clean saucepan and reduce until it has a good strong flavour and use as required.

Note 1: If making brown chicken stock it should simmer for about 4 hours – brown beef stock should simmer for about 6 hours. Fish stock however should only be simmered for about 30 minutes, after that the flavour becomes bitter.

Note 2: Stock can be reduced to a glaze by boiling it until it is very tacky and then freezing it in ice cube trays. Defrost the cubes as required and dilute with water to get the correct flavour.

Roasted Spice Mix

2 cinnamon sticks, halved

20g coriander seeds

35g cumin seeds

28g fennel seeds

55g mustard seeds

55g fenugreek seeds

5 cardamom pods

3 star anise

1.   Place a non–stick pan over a low heat and when it begins to smoke slightly add all the spices.

2.   Cook, stirring frequently, until the seeds just begin to pop. It is important not to burn the spices.

3.   Leave to get completely cold and then grind, ideally in a pestle and mortar, to a fine powder. If you don't have a pestle and mortar use a coffee grinder or liquidiser – the Magimix will not grind the spices finely enough.

4.   Store in an airtight container.

Note: The quantities of spices required may seem unusual but they are the most common supermarket pack sizes of the different spices.

Yorkshire Puddings

Makes 8

100g plain flour

pinch of salt

2 medium eggs, beaten

275ml milk, or a mixture of milk and water

60g goose or duck fat, melted or 60ml vegetable oil

The traditional accompaniment to roast beef, these are best baked while the joint is resting. Prepare the batter in advance.

Stages 1–3 can also be made by placing the flour, eggs, milk and water and salt into a Magimix and blitzing until just smooth. Leave to stand for 40 minutes or so – the mixture must have no bubbles before baking.

1. Sift the flour and salt into a bowl and make a well in the centre. Pour the eggs into the well.

2. Stir the eggs with a wooden spoon, concentrating your stirring only in the eggs, gradually drawing in flour from around the edge. Don't force flour in; it will be incorporated automatically as you stir the eggs.

3. As the egg mixture becomes thicker, add a little milk to loosen it, then keep stirring. Continue in this way until all the flour has been incorporated. Beat to ensure the thick mixture is smooth before adding the remaining milk. Chill the batter in the refrigerator for at least 30 minutes.

4. Heat the oven to 220C/425F, gas mark 7.

5. Spoon a little fat into 8 moulds of a deep muffin tin (ideally non-stick); there should only be about 2mm fat in the bottom of each mould. Swirl the fat so that the sides of the moulds are lightly greased. Place the tin on a baking tray in the oven to heat.

6. When the fat is very hot, test a few drops of batter in one well; the oil should sizzle, so if it doesn't, return the tin to the oven to heat. Quickly fill the muffin moulds about half full with the batter and return to the oven immediately. Cook for 25–30 minutes until well risen, a deep golden colour and crisp on the outside. Do not open the oven door during baking, or the puddings may collapse.

7. Remove from the oven, unmould each pudding and drain on a tray lined with kitchen paper, then serve at once.

Notes

To Joint a Raw Chicken

1. Singe the chicken then wipe with kitchen paper to remove any hairs and pin feathers.

2. Place the chicken on a red board (see Safety Advice on p.174) breast side down with the Parson's nose facing you.

3. Using a large cook's knife make a cut down the backbone through the skin from one end to the other.

4. Use your thumbs to loosen the oyster pieces located at the top of each leg next to the backbone.

5. Turn the chicken over, pull up the skin tightly over the breast then cut between the breast and the leg, cutting as close to the leg as possible using the blade of the knife, not the tip.

6. Continue cutting the skin around the leg to the backbone next to the oyster piece.

7. Bend the leg out from the body to release the ball joint from the socket.

8. Use a knife to cut the cartilage around the ball joint.

9. Remove the leg by grasping it firmly and pulling it towards the back of the chicken. The oyster piece should come away with the leg.

10. Repeat steps 5–9 to remove the other leg.

11. Feel for the joint between the drumstick and the thigh then cut through the joint using a large knife.

12. Place the chicken breast side up on the board then cut through the breast meat of the chicken from one end to the other using the blade of the knife.

13. Using scissors cut through the breastbone and wishbone. Do not remove the breastbone from the breast meat. Cut out the wishbone.

14. Using scissors cut along the fat line on the edge of the breast, cutting through the ends of the ribs then around underneath the wing to the neck of the chicken. Save the carcass for stock.

15. Tuck the wings back into the 'sunbathing position'. Place the two breasts next to each other then cut through the meat on a slant from the 'elbow' to the 'cleavage'.

16.   After cooking use scissors to remove the pinion (wing tip) from each wing. Remove the knuckles by grasping the end with kitchen paper then cutting through the skin with a knife, then using scissors push the skin back and cut through the bone. Use scissors to remove any other unsightly bits of bone from the chicken pieces.

To Joint a Cooked Chicken

The principle of how to joint a cooked chicken is fairly similar to jointing raw chicken but because the chicken has been cooked you should use a carving knife and fork rather than touching the chicken with your hands.

1.   Place the chicken breast side up on a brown board (see Safety Advice on p.174) with the Parson's nose away from you.

2.   Carefully carve between the breast and leg keeping as close to the leg as possible. Let the leg fall sideways and try to separate it from the main part of the bird. Remove the leg. Repeat with the other leg. Turn the leg skin-side down and looking carefully for a slightly defined fat line carve the joint in half, separating the leg and thigh. Remove the knuckle. Place skin-side up on the serving dish.

3.   Cut the wing joints off with a generous amount of breast. Remove the wing tips.

4.   Remove both sides of the breast from the breast bone.

To Skin and Fillet a Flat Fish

Cleaning the fish

Flat fish are usually sold gutted but it is a good idea to rinse and pat the fish dry before preparing it.

Removing the head

Mark the head with a sharp knife and then using a pair of scissors cut off the head.

To skin the dark side

Note: This method is not very suitable for lemon sole and I would recommend skinning after filleting (see To skin the white side below).

Place the fish on a piece of greaseproof paper and have a little pile of table salt to hand (this will help when you need to grip the fish).

Place the fish on the paper with the tail facing you.

Make a crossway slit through the skin at the tail and push your finger under the skin. Run your finger around the edge of the fish, loosening all of the skin.

When you have done this on both edges, salt your fingers and take a firm grip of the skin at the tail end with one hand and with the other hold the fish down. Give a strong yank, peeling the skin back towards the head end and remove it in one piece.

The white side of the fish is generally tenderer and should be removed once the fish has been filleted.

To fillet a flat fish

Lay the fish on the board with the tail towards you. Cut through the flesh to the backbone along the length of the fish. With a sharp pliable knife cut the fillet away from the bone – the fillet is almost stroked off the bone. You should hear the sound of your knife against the bone as you remove the fillet. Use bold strokes.

Swivel the fish around so that the head end is towards you and remove the second fillet in exactly the same way.

Turn the fish over and repeat on the other side. If you are left handed it may be easier to tackle the right hand fillet first.

If you come across any roe keep it whole – it is delicious fried gently and served on buttered toast.

To skin the white side

Place the fillet on the board with the thin end towards you.

Using a sharp flexible knife carefully lift the fillet off the skin. The knife should be at an angle of about 25 degrees and as you lift the fillet away you need to pull the skin towards you.

Trim all the fillets neatly using a pair of scissors.

Deep-Fat Frying

Deep-fat frying makes for delicious food but it can be dangerous so follow these safety tips:

- Never leave a fat fryer unattended – the fat can burst into flames if the fryer gets too hot.

- Never move a deep-fryer.

- Always have a fire blanket nearby.

- Always have a lid close by – fire needs oxygen to survive so if the fat gets too hot put a lid on the fryer – never douse it with water.

- Should the fryer burst into flames turn off the heat source.

- Never fill a fryer more than two-thirds full of fat and always make sure that the food you add to the fryer is well dried.

To Scale, Gut and Fillet a Round Fish

Scaling

1. Put the fish (head first) into a large plastic bag and using the blunt side of the knife scrape off the scales from the tail end. (Most of the scales should stay in the bag.) Remove the fish and discard the bag.

2. Rinse the fish and pat dry.

Gutting

3. Using scissors cut off all the fins – except for the dorsal fin (the big one in the middle of the back).

4. Remove the gills – this is best done using scissors.

5. Put your hand on top of the fish (this helps to keep the belly taut) and carefully cut through the belly of the fish from the vent hole to just near the head of the fish. Don't cut too deeply or you may cut into the guts.

6. Open the belly and remove all the guts – it may be necessary to cut some of them out. Using a teaspoon scrape out the blood from the backbone.

7. Rinse well and pat dry.

Filleting

8. Make a cut across the fish at an angle below the gill flap and fin to the belly.

9. Make a shallow cut from behind the head along the top of the dorsal fin to the tail.

10. Using long sweeping strokes gradually free the top fillet from the bones. Release the fillet and turn the fish over. The second fillet is a little trickier to do but proceed as per the first fillet.

11. Trim off any excess fatty skin.

12. Carefully pin bone the fillets using kitchen tweezers.

Lining a Flan Ring

Sprinkle a little flour over both the work surface and the rolling pin.

Roll out the pastry into a circle about 2cm larger than your chosen flan ring. As you roll turn the pastry several times to prevent it from sticking to the work surface.

Drape the pastry onto the rolling pin, lift it up and carefully let it drop over the flan ring.

Using your fingers very gently ease the pastry into the ring and push it into place, trying not to get any creases in the pastry. If you have rolled the pastry into too large a circle it becomes cumbersome to work with – on the other hand you don't want to stretch the pastry either.

Using the rolling pin, roll off the excess pastry – the sharpness of the flan ring will cut the pastry.

Refrigerate until firm.

Note: I always recommend using a metal flan ring placed on a baking sheet rather than using a ceramic flan dish as you will get a crisper pastry.

Baking Blind

If a recipe calls for the pastry to be baked blind pre-heat the oven to 200C/400F, gas mark 6 or 190C/375F, gas mark 5 for sweet pastry.

Cut out a circle of greaseproof paper a little larger than the flan ring, crumple it up in your hands and then use it to line the flan ring.

Fill the pastry with enough baking blind beans or rice to support the sides of the pastry. The base needs only a fine layer of beans or rice.

Bake for 15 minutes or until the sides are firm. Remove the beans, cover the sides of the pastry with a strip of aluminium foil and then bake until the pastry is a pale biscuit colour and feels sandy.

Note: The beans or rice can be used again and again but if using rice make sure that it is completely cold before storing in a sealed container.

Using Gelatine

Gelatine comes in powder or leaf form. It can be a little tricky to use so I have included a few tips:

Powder gelatine

Place water in a saucepan (normally 3 tablespoons), sprinkle over the gelatine called for and leave it to 'sponge' for 3 minutes. Melt it over a very gentle heat until clear and runny. Do not stir or boil.

Add the gelatine to a mixture that is at room temperature and do not add any further ingredients such as whisked egg white or cream until the mixture is nearly at the point of setting.

Leaf gelatine

If a recipe calls for powdered gelatine and you want to use leaf, substitute 1 leaf for every teaspoon of powdered gelatine. The general rule for a jelly is that you need 1 leaf of supermarket gelatine for every 100ml of liquid.

Soak the gelatine in cold water for 5 minutes. Make sure that all the gelatine is covered. Do not soak for any longer as it will begin to dissolve. Squeeze the gelatine to remove excess water.

For adding to cold ingredients: put enough water into a saucepan to cover the base of the pan and bring it up to the boil. Add the squeezed gelatine and remove from the heat. Allow the gelatine to melt completely and then use as required.

For adding to tepid liquids: add the squeezed gelatine to the warm liquid and allow it to dissolve.

Sourdough Notes

Making a sourdough loaf is more time consuming than making normal bread but well worth the effort. It also keeps much better than a conventional loaf.

You will need a starter – it is possible to make your own but my first one came from Hobbs House Bakery in Bath and was excellent. I now have one given to me by Peter Gordon and it is even better. The starter should be kept in the fridge at all times.

Once you have the starter you will need to look after it. If you are making bread daily you can just feed it every day. Feed the starter, return it to the fridge and then use when it passes the float test. (See below.) It should be kept in something like a Kilner jar – it should not be absolutely airtight so remove the band before use.

Feeding a starter

There are many slightly contradictory methods of feeding a starter. I simply mix together three parts rye flour to four parts flat mineral water to a smooth paste. The paste should be just under half of the volume of the starter in the jar – it is not an exact science and you get to know your own starter and begin to feed it what you feel it needs. Mix the paste with some of your starter then pour this mixture into the jar and stir well. The starter is not ready for use until it is hungry again – I generally feed my starter at night and it is ready for use the following morning.

A starter can be kept in the fridge for up to 3 weeks without feeding; it may then have a pool of grey liquid on the top – tip most of the liquid away and then feed the starter – it may need several feeds before it is ready and can take up to two days before it passes the float test.

The float test

To check that a fed starter is ready for use it should look bubbly. Then drop a small teaspoonful of starter into a mug of water – if it floats for at least 20 seconds it is ready for use. It is important to test once the water is absolutely still – if there is a tiny vortex the starter will sink. If you do need to do the float test more than once use a clean mug of water – if you use the same water again sometimes the starter will sink immediately.

If you find that it doesn't float, having left the starter overnight add a small amount of rye flour mixed with water to a smooth paste as before and about 2 hours later it should pass the float test. It may be that it had passed the critical point and was getting 'hungry' again.

Roasting Tables

- Weigh the joint and establish the length of cooking time (see below).

- Preheat the oven (electric ovens take longer to heat up than gas ovens).

- Prepare the joint for roasting; see the relevant recipe.

- Allow the meat to stand for at least 15 minutes at room temperature before carving. This allows the fibre of the meat to relax and absorb some of the juices.

These tables are guidelines only – a long thin piece of meat will cook more quickly than a short fat piece of the same weight. Meat on the bone tends to cook more quickly than a boned joint of the same weight as bones are good conductors of heat. A meat thermometer can help you decide if the meat is cooked – generally rare meat reaches an internal temperature of 52C/126F; 60C/140F to be medium. Beef is generally cooked at 220C/425F, gas mark 7 for 20 minutes or browned all over in a pan before being put into the oven. Whatever the method, the cooking time is after the initial browning.

		°C	°F	Gas	per kg	per lb
Beef	Rare roast	180	350	4	25 mins	10 mins
	Medium roast	180	350	4	40 mins	15 mins
Pork		190	375	5	55 mins	25 mins
Lamb		190	375	5	45 mins	20 mins

		°C	°F	Gas	per kg	per lb
Chicken		200	400	6	45 mins	20 mins
Turkey	Under 6k	200	400	6	30 mins	12 mins
	Large	180	350	4	35 mins	15 mins
Duck		200	400	6	35 mins	15 mins
Goose		190	375	5	30 mins	12 mins
Pigeon		200	400	6	12–15 minutes	
Grouse		200	400	6	15–20 minutes	
Partridge		200	400	6	25 minutes	
Pheasant		190	375	5	30 minutes	
Guinea Fowl		190	375	5	70 minutes	

Very small birds need to be browned all over in a frying pan before roasting – they need such a short cooking time that they would not get brown enough if simply roasted. Cook them at 200C/400F, gas mark 6.

Small Birds

Woodcock	10 minutes in total
Quail	15 minutes in total
Snipe	12 minutes in total

Note: Few chickens, however small. will cook in less than an hour and few turkeys, however small, will cook in less than 2 hours.

General Notes

These are notes of the tips that you have been given during your cookery course at Dudwell School:

- **Sharpening a knife** – the angle should be about 25/30° to the steel – always draw the blade of the knife away from your body, sharpen away from food and sharpen every time you use a knife.

- **Presentation:** keep it simple, aim for centre height, use relevant and edible garnish, and think about colour, use uneven numbers as far as possible. If arranging, say, a tomato and mozzarella salad make sure that the tomatoes and cheese are sliced to the same thickness and arrange them in even overlapping slices. If arranging cutlets on a dish make sure that all the bones are facing the same direction. If food looks nice people assume that it tastes good.

- When **chopping** get a flat surface as quickly as you can – this way you are less likely to chop yourself. Chopping an onion – keep the root intact – it will stop you crying too much. Do two or three horizontal cuts and then as many vertical as you can and then chop using your knuckles as a guard. Place the chopping board on a damp J-cloth – it keeps it in place.

- Make a wet **cartouche** for sweating vegetables in order to prevent them from burning.

- Always **preheat the oven**. An electric oven generally takes longer to get to the right temperature than a gas oven.

- Always **fry or grill** the side of the food you want to serve uppermost first – the second side never looks so good. When frying meat the less you move it the better – it will lift easily once it is ready to move.

- Green **vegetables** are cooked, uncovered, in boiling salted water. Vegetables that are grown underground are generally put into cold salted water; bring the water up to the boil, cover and then simmer until tender.

- **Season** food at the beginning of the cooking process and then adjust the seasoning at the end. Pulses are the exception to the rule.

- When making **shortcrust pastry** the important technique is rubbing the fat into the flour – this coats the flour with fat which protects the flour and hinders the development of gluten which would make the pastry tough.

- When a recipe says **beat** it means use a wooden spoon – if it says **whisk** use a whisk. Always add thinner mixtures to thicker mixtures. When beating or whisking, place the bowl on a damp J-cloth – it holds it in place.

- When working with **yeast** remember yeast needs warmth, moisture and food to work so use warm water and add a little sugar. Yeast is killed by excessive heat and by too much salt. Knead a bread **dough** until it looks spongy. Generally the first kneading will take about 5–10 minutes of vigorous handling. Press the dough with your finger – it should spring back into the original place.

- **Quiche** mixtures must be cooked at a moderate temperature or the mixture will curdle.

- Use granulated sugar for **sugar syrups and caramel sauce** – it must dissolve before you bring the mixture to the boil. It is dissolved when the liquid has become completely clear. If the water is allowed to boil before the sugar has dissolved, sugar crystals will begin to form. Sugar crystals attract more sugar crystals.

- Use a serrated-edge knife for **fruit** preparation.

- When **frying mince** add a few chopped onions to help break up the mince and fry using a fork – this helps to prevent lumpy mince. Mince needs to be cooked slowly for at least 2 hours – never add flour to mince – it should become syrupy rather than gluggy. Cook it with plenty of red wine. If it looks greasy you can use absorbent paper to soak away some of the fat. Adding a little milk can help as it seems to absorb fat.

- To check that **mussels** are alive – the shells should be shut. If they are not tap them lightly on the work surface and if they still don't shut discard. Also discard any that are unusually heavy. Once cooked discard any mussels that remain shut.

- **Ice cream** needs to be whisked a great deal to get a good consistency – an ice cream machine means that you can make truly high quality ice cream at home – it is worth spending money on a good machine.

- **French dressing** is normally 3 parts oil to 1 part vinegar but if using very good olive oil and balsamic vinegar use 5 parts oil to 1 part vinegar. If you like a thick dressing use mustard to emulsify and thicken.

- **To peel tomatoes** prick them lightly with a sharp knife and put into a bowl. Pour over boiling water and leave to stand for 5 seconds. Remove from the water with a slotted spoon and peel. If the skin does not come off easily, return to the bowl for a further 5 seconds.

- **To peel ginger** use the sharp edge of a teaspoon. Ginger can be kept in the freezer – grating frozen ginger is much easier than grating fresh ginger. You will need to use double the quantity of ginger called for in the recipe as the frozen ginger will contain water.

- Always **crush garlic** on a piece of greaseproof paper to protect the board from smelling of garlic. If using a garlic crusher simply place the unskinned garlic clove in the crusher and squeeze. The skin stays in the crusher.

- **Chocolate** melts at a low temperature so when melting it place the bowl over, not in, a pan of simmering water and then turn the heat off and allow the chocolate to melt. I would always use Green and Blacks cooking chocolate – non-cooking chocolate is difficult to work with and many cooking chocolates are very nasty.

- **Choux pastry** is made in a completely different way to other pastry as it benefits from vigorous beating. The most important thing is to measure the ingredients very accurately. The panade (flour, butter and water mixture) should be cool before you add the eggs. When baking choux, if the buns look cooked give them an extra 5 minutes in the oven – pierce them with a skewer so that the inside can dry out a little. Always add sweetened cream to profiteroles and make sure they are well filled. If piping in cream fill the bag carefully and avoid getting any air pockets.

- **Pancake batters** should be allowed to stand for 30 minutes to allow the starch cells time to expand – this means that they will burst when they are cooked and you can guarantee very thin light crepes.

- **To prepare asparagus** snap them in your hand and discard the short piece.

- When **poaching fish** leave the skin – this helps to protect the fish. You can tell when the fish is cooked as the skin will be easy to remove. Reserve the poaching liquor to make a sauce.

- When making a **white sauce** add a little extra butter as this will make it shiny. Melt the butter. Remove from heat, add the flour – return to a low heat and cook for 1 minute but do not allow the flour to colour. Remove from the heat and gradually add the milk, stirring all the time. Return to the heat and bring slowly up to the boil, stirring continually. Simmer for a minute or two. Invest in a sauce whisk.

- Think about buying a **salad spinner** – much the best way to dry lettuce.

- **Onions** take at least 45 minutes to sweat until really soft – use a cartouche.

- When making **mint sauce**, chop the mint with a little sugar. It makes it faster and easier to chop.

- Adding water to an **omelette** makes it lighter than it would be without the addition of water.

- **Brownies** can be frozen and when defrosted they are fudgier and better than before.

- Use '00' wheat flour to make **pasta**. 00 means the flour has been very finely milled. Do not add salt to pasta: it can result in white patches in the dough. An electric pasta machine is much more efficient than a manual machine.

- **Pesto** is simple to make and much nicer than the bought variety.

- As soon as you have added liquid to flour with a **raising agent** in it the mixture should be baked as soon as possible. Liquid and heat activate the raising agent.

- Don't fill a **sushi** roll too full. To mould the rice, wet your hands in cold water that has a little vinegar in it. When using pickled ginger squeeze it well before serving.

- All **roast meat** must be allowed to rest before carving and this is particularly important for tender cuts such as duck breasts. Score the breasts, salt them and fry, skin-side down, in a little oil until well browned, reduce the heat and allow to cook slowly, so as to render down some of the fat. Turn over and place on a wire rack (to allow for good circulation of heat) on a roasting tin and cook for about 10 minutes and then rest for a further four minutes before slicing. This gives the juices time to set a little, which means that the meat becomes very tender.

- A good **cheese soufflé** is easy to make but timing is critical so all mise en place (preperation) must be done before starting to cook. Prepare the soufflé dishes – brush with melted butter and dust with dried white breadcrumbs. Make the cheese sauce – follow the rules of making a white sauce and then remove from the heat and add the grated cheese. Allow the cheese to melt without returning the sauce to the heat. Tip into a large bowl. Add the egg yolks. Whisk the whites until stiff but not dry. (Remember not to separate an egg over an already separated white.) Beat a spoonful of the whites into the sauce to loosen the mixture then fold in the rest using a cutting and folding action with a large metal spoon. Pile into the prepared dishes – they should be almost full. Run your finger around the top of the mixture (to create a good top hat) and tap the dish lightly on the work top (to remove any pockets of air). Place in the preheated oven.

- **Mayonnaise** is an emulsion sauce and it is easy to curdle it. Beat the yolks well with mustard (a good emulsifier) and salt, add the oil drip by drip until the mixture is quite thick. Add a little of the lemon juice or vinegar and then add the remaining oil with more confidence. Should it curdle, place an egg yolk in a clean bowl, beat well, and then gradually add the curdled mixture.

- **Meringues** are best made using a good quality machine whisk. Whisk the egg whites until stiff but not dry. With the machine still running add half the sugar in spoonfuls in a period of one and a half minutes. Add the remaining sugar and whisk for a couple of seconds. Spoon onto 'Bake-O-Glide' paper placed on a baking sheet. Meringues are dried out rather than cooked. When cold, place in a well-sealed tin. Store in a dry place – not the refrigerator. The paper is reusable.

- If you put a **mango** on a work surface it will always land with the stone running parallel to the work surface.

- **Squid** must be cooked in a matter of minutes – if overcooked it will become tough.

- **Eggs** are very versatile; on the whole yolks are for enriching and thickening (e.g. hollandaise sauce) and whites are for setting and for lightening (e.g. lemon soufflé).

- **Useful gadgets**: potato ricer, microplane, sauce whisk, mango cutter.

- **Hollandaise** – can be time consuming to make – I would always recommend making it in a food processor (see recipe on page 88). If by chance it curdles try adding either a little bit of ice or a drop of boiling water – if this doesn't work start again with a new egg yolk and treat the curdled mixture as the butter.

- **Vanilla sugar** can be made by placing a vanilla pod in a jar of caster sugar. As the sugar is used, top up the jar with more caster sugar.

- **Vanish** can be used to clean stubborn pan stains.

- **Chillies** – if you burn yourself apply milk not water.

- When cleaning boards on which **fish** has been prepared use cold water first – hot water will cook the fish onto the board. Always soak pans using cold water.

- Never cover ingredients that are cooling down – it means that they stay hot for a longer time than if uncovered – to prevent food poisoning all food should be cooled down as quickly as possible. Try not to put hot food into the fridge as this raises the temperature of the fridge.

- When deciding how to **cook a piece of meat** the basic principle is to think where it is on the body of the animal. The more it moves (e.g. oxtail) the slower and longer it needs to cook. The less it moves (e.g. fillet) the quicker and faster it needs to be cooked. The collagen in the connective tissue in cuts of meat such as oxtail is converted into gelatine, making the cut very tender indeed.

- Only **stuff a turkey** at the neck end. Stuffing the cavity can make you vulnerable to food poisoning.

- Always **stretch bacon** on the back of a knife before cooking – this is because it tends to shrink and if stretched it simply goes back to its original size. The best way to cook bacon such as pancetta is to stretch and place it on a baking sheet and cook it in a hot oven for 10 minutes or so.

- **Mustard** is a great emulsifier.

Time Plans

A time plan should be an ORDER OF WORK. It should enable the student to follow a programme of work that is both efficient and effective without too much reference to the recipe books. This can be achieved by taking the following into account.

1.   **Menu:** Write down what is to be cooked, the page numbers and the quantities.

2.   **Collect ingredients:** This section should be ingredients bracketed together into each individual recipe so that it can be easy to see what they are for. The quantities should be included so that they need not be repeated later in the cooking section.

3.   **Mise en place:** (literally to put into place) In a restaurant this would include all the vegetable and meat preparation, chopping of herbs etc. However, at school, because of time constraints, whichever job takes the longest should be done first. Do jobs of the same type together, e.g. if onions need to be chopped for more than one recipe do them all at the same time.

4.   **Cooking:** This will note down the order that the food is being prepared and cooked. With a recipe that has not been attempted before more detail can be added, but once it has become familiar the instruction can become less detailed.
     E.g. Make the white sauce, melt butter in a saucepan, add flour and stir over the heat for one minute. Take off the heat and gradually add cold milk. Put the pan back on the heat and bring gradually to the boil, then add the remaining milk. Boil for at least two minutes.
     Or
     Make the white sauce using butter, flour and milk.

5.   **Reminders:** Put in reminders to wash up, clear up and empty the rubbish bin – it is easy to forget.

6.   **Timings:** There can be helpful timings, e.g. put in the oven by 11.25am or don't put in the oven before 11.25am but don't put timings for every single item. Remember to adjust the timings if cooking smaller quantities.

7.   **Highlight:** A highlighter pen can be used, for example, when you want to keep a check on food, and a column at the side of the page can help with this, e.g. onions sweating, check bread, stock etc.

8.   **Service list:** Useful if you need to collect plates to be warmed or if some food is not to be served until the next day. There may be food from the day before to be served.

Safety Advice

GENERAL

1.   Please note fire exit routes. The fire assembly point is on the first terrace.

2.   Please note where all fire extinguishers are situated and watch CW demonstrate how to use a fire blanket. She will also instruct you on the use of the fire extinguishers.

3.   Please let CW know of anything that I should know about you (e.g. epileptic, pregnant, diabetic, allergies etc.) before cooking. CW has an allergen register of all food used on the course.

4.   Please note the position of the first aid box.

5.   Please wipe your feet thoroughly when entering the building with wet shoes.

6.   Please don't lock your bedrooms at night – to enable a quick exit in case of fire.

7.   All doors in the building should be kept closed at all times.

KITCHEN

1.   Wash hands thoroughly before cooking and when changing tasks.
     Use alcoholic gel on a regular basis.

2.   Avoid touching cooked foods with your hands.

3.   Use the right coloured boards:
     a.   Red – raw foods
     b.   Brown – cooked food and raw food requiring no further cooking (e.g. chopped parsley).

4.   Do not turn on cookers or use knives unless CW is in the room.

5.   If anything is spilt on the floor please wipe it up immediately. If anything is dropped on the floor that you might trip over clear it up immediately.

6.   Put all breakages into sharps bins.

7.   No hot items in rubbish sacks.

8. Don't use tea towels to remove hot pans from the oven.

9. Never leave glasses or knives in the sinks.

10. Call out 'hot pan' when transporting hot items from the cooker.

11. Never walk around the kitchen pointing a knife at anyone. Carry knives at your side with the blade pointing down.

12. Don't lean on the cooker.

13. Turn off gas rings and cookers when you have finished with them.

14. Don't put anything, other than saucepans, on the cookers (e.g. not the plastic trays). Only touch plugs with dry hands.

15. Always turn off switches before removing or inserting plugs.

16. No one can come into the kitchen with diarrhoea or vomiting until they have been clear of the symptoms for 48 hours.

17. If you notice that anything is unsafe, report it to CW and do not use it.

18. Matches should always be kept beside the grill – CW will point out the exact place – this is a fire safety issue.

FIRST AID

BURNS: hold affected area under running cold water – an ice pack may be necessary.

CUTS: ask CW for immediate first aid.

OUTSIDE

All outside equipment is used at your own risk. The trampoline is not to be used. The swimming pool can only be used when supervised by CW or WAW. No diving is allowed. No swimming allowed if alcohol has been consumed. No swimming in poor light unless the pool lights have been turned on.

Take care when leaving the big barn – there is a small step that you may not notice.

Dudwell School Recipe Pack Index